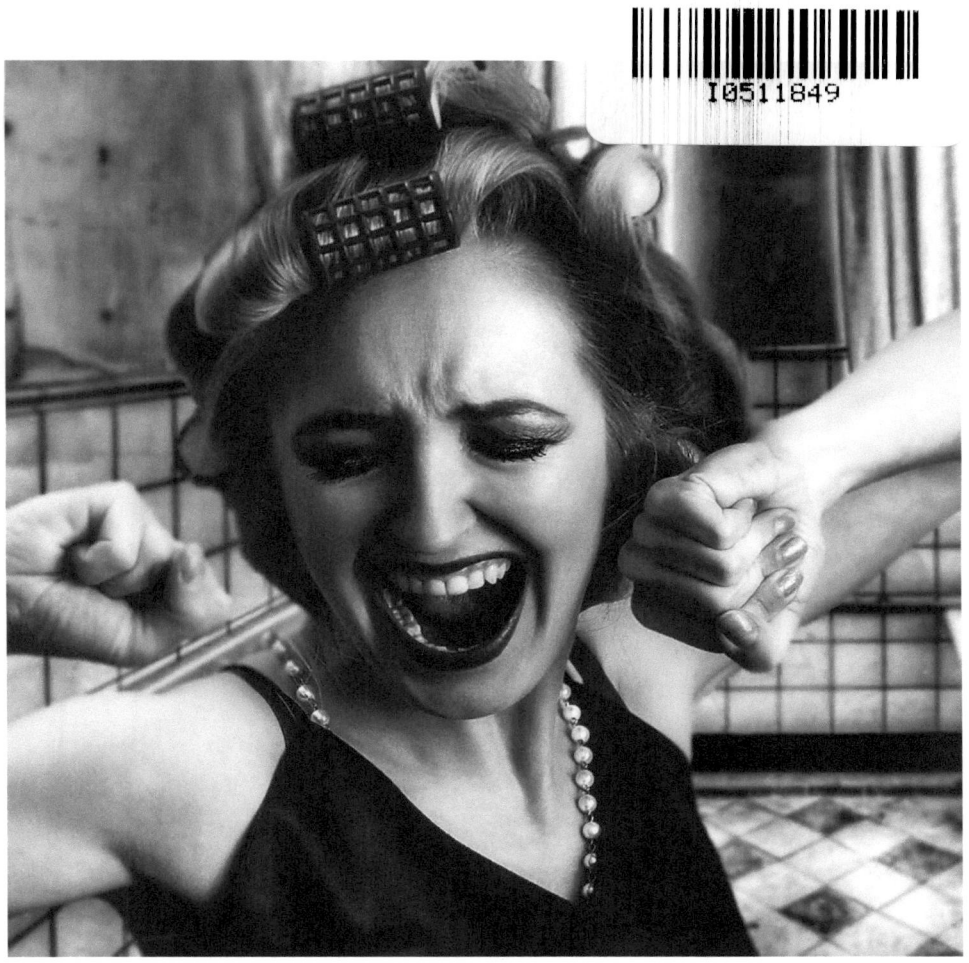

Every day struggle..
# WHAT HAIR STYLE FOR TODAY?

THIS BOOK BELONGS TO
**EMYZO CREATURES
EDITION**

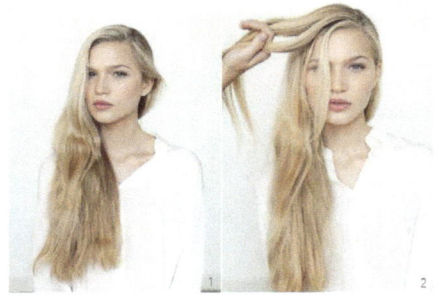
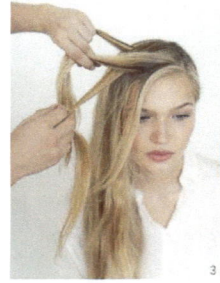
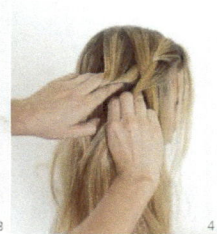
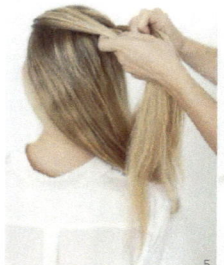
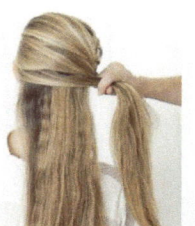

**Let's start with some stylish braids**

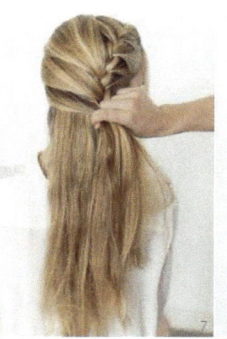
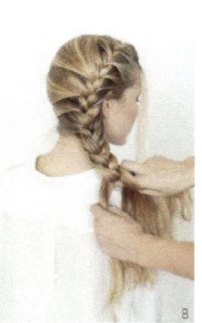
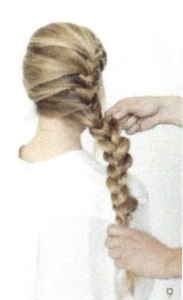
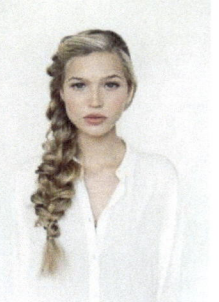

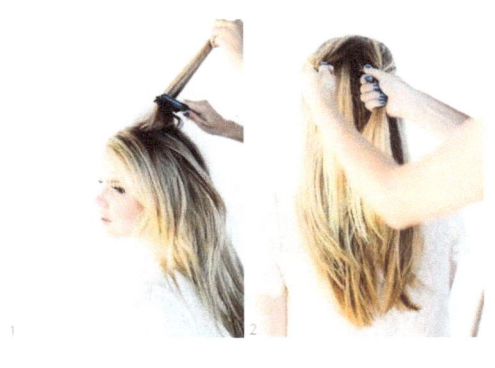

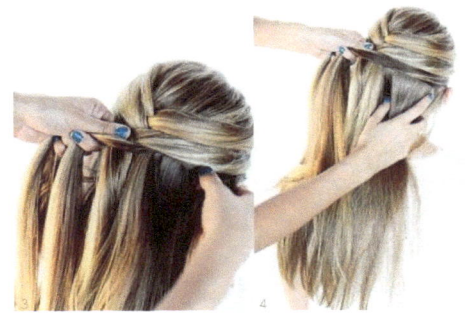

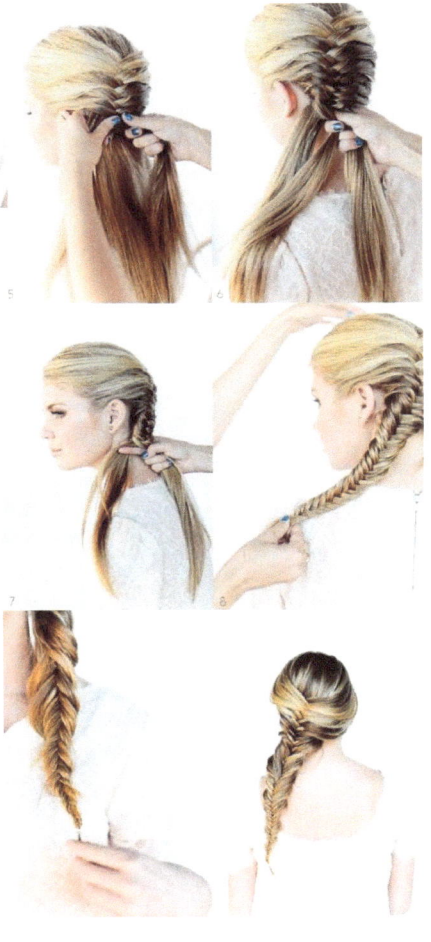

Having someone braids your hair is a blessing

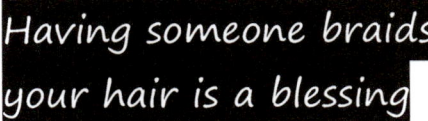

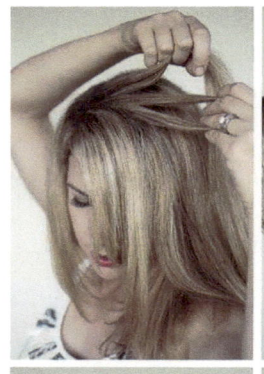 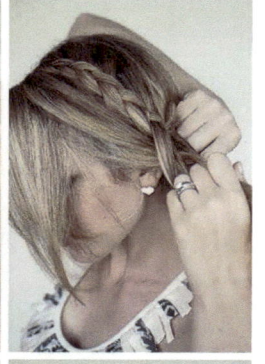 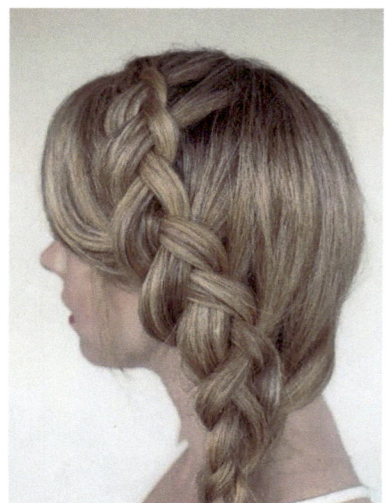

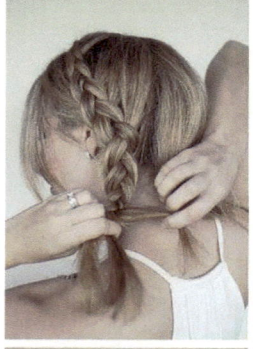 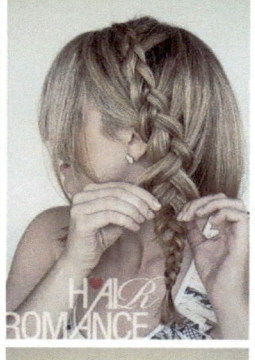

## Dutch side mermaid braid

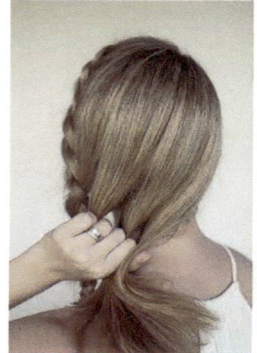 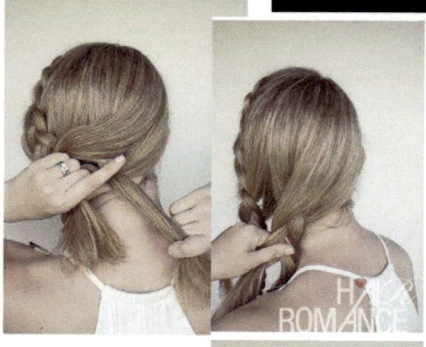 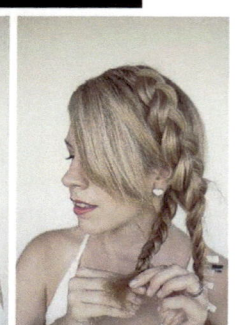

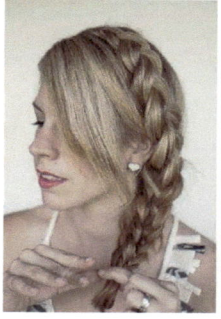 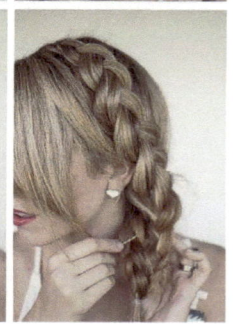

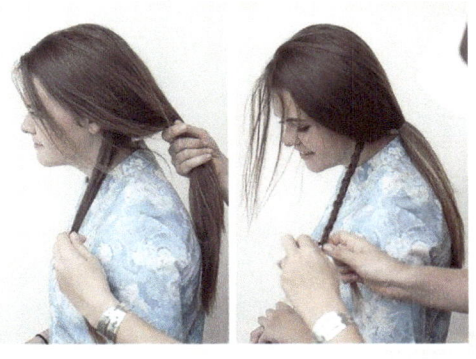

Braid in a side braid

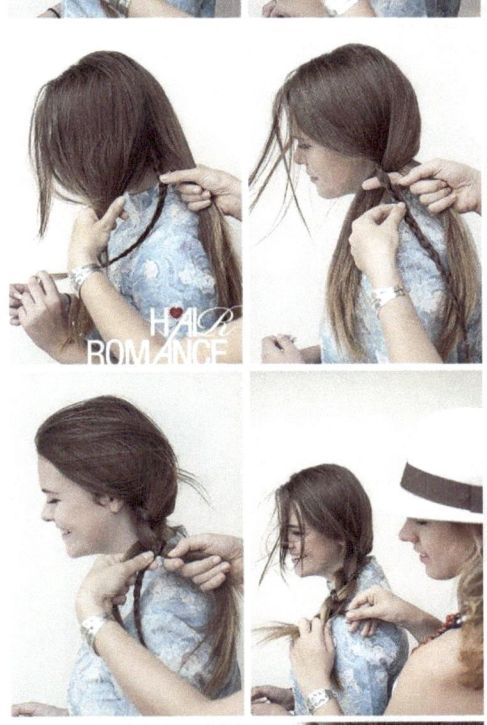
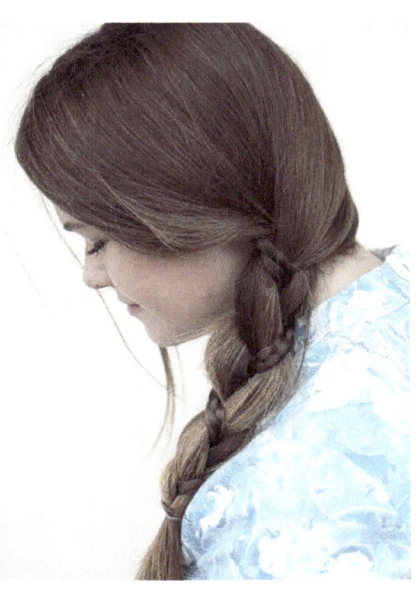
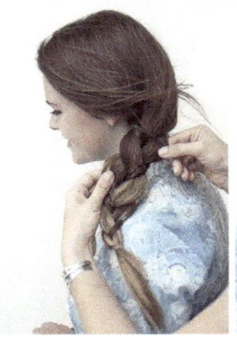
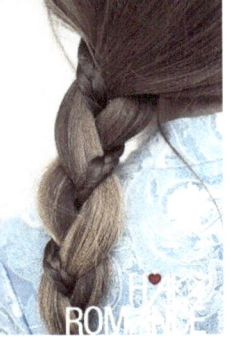

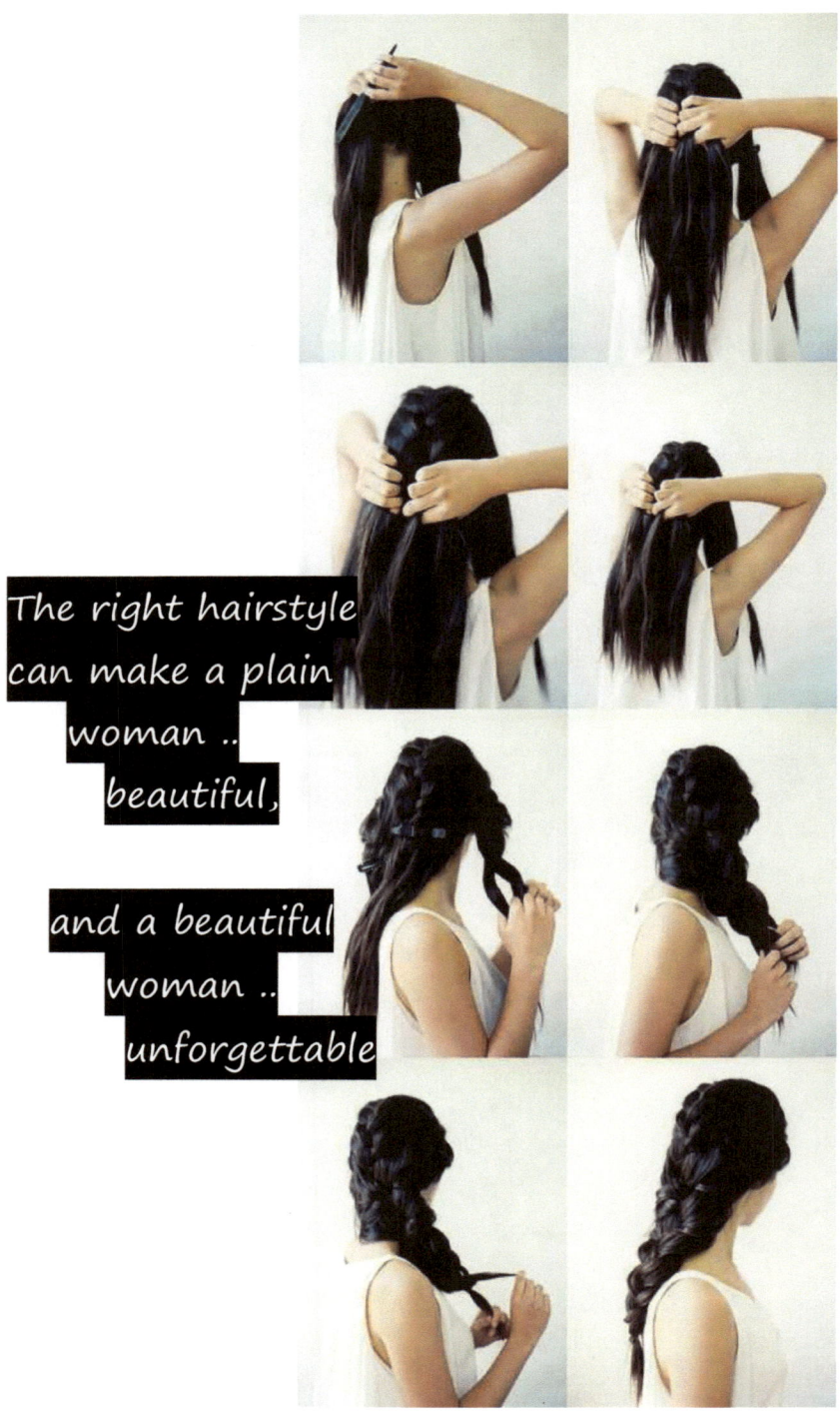

The right hairstyle can make a plain woman .. beautiful, and a beautiful woman .. unforgettable

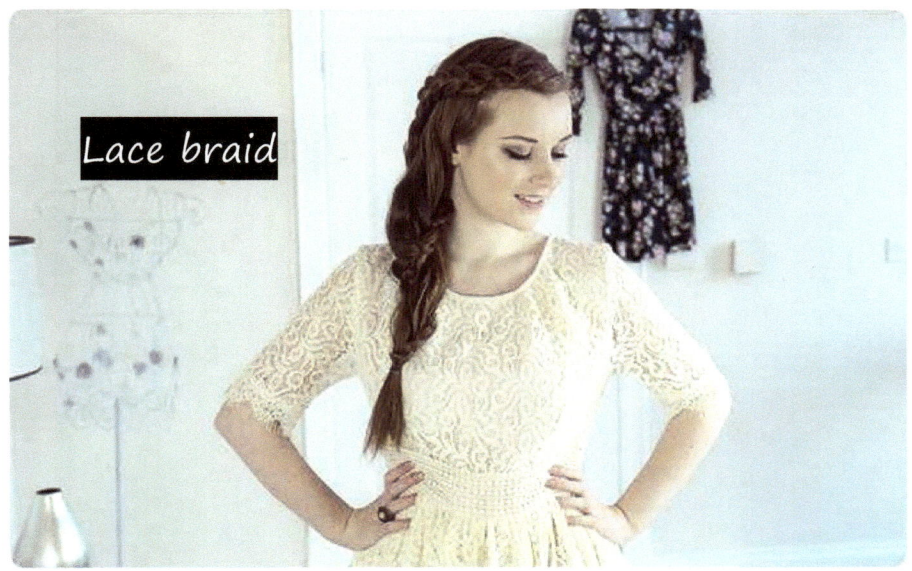

**Lace braid**

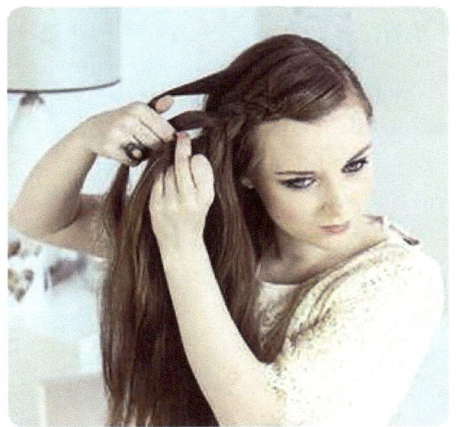
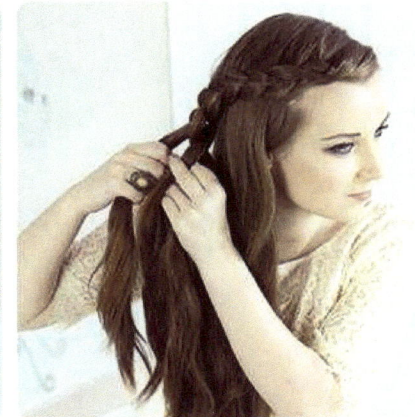
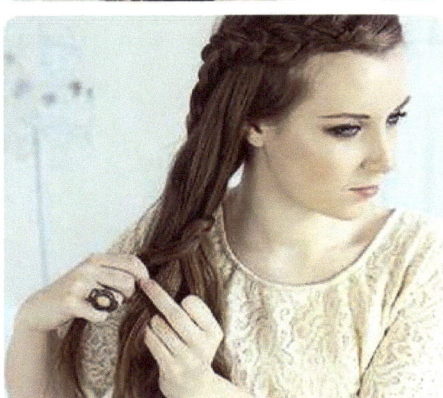
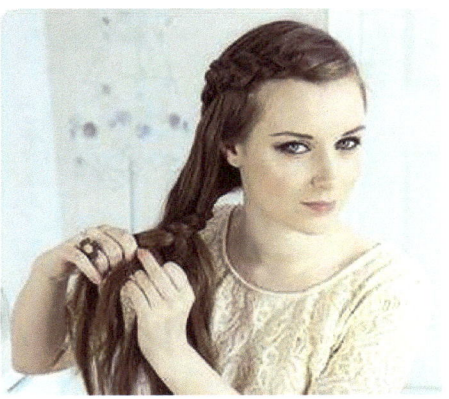

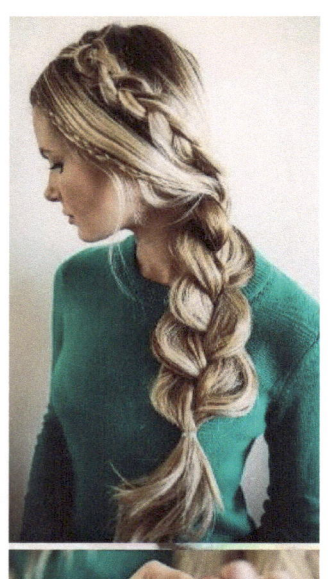
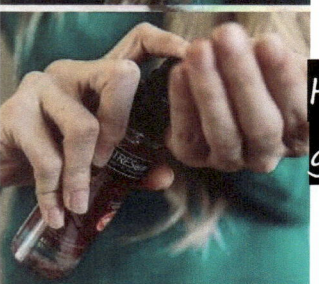

Happiness is a good hair day

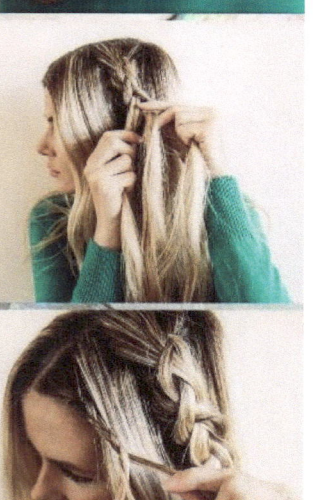
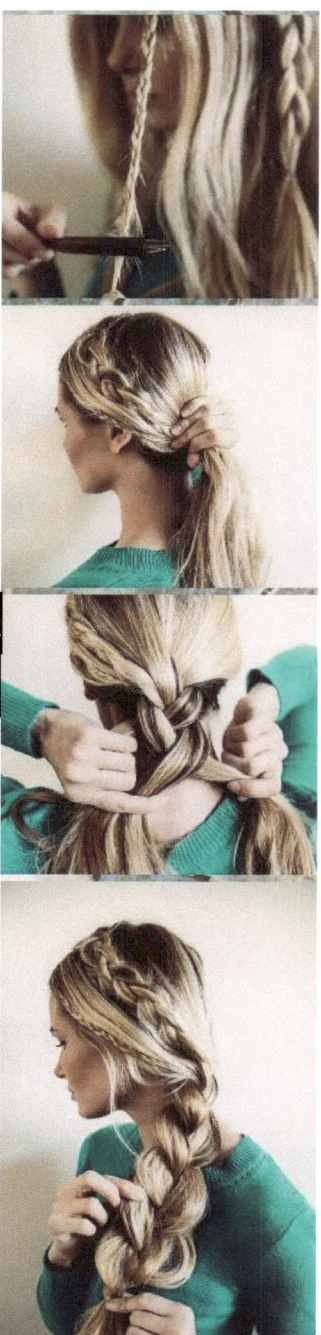

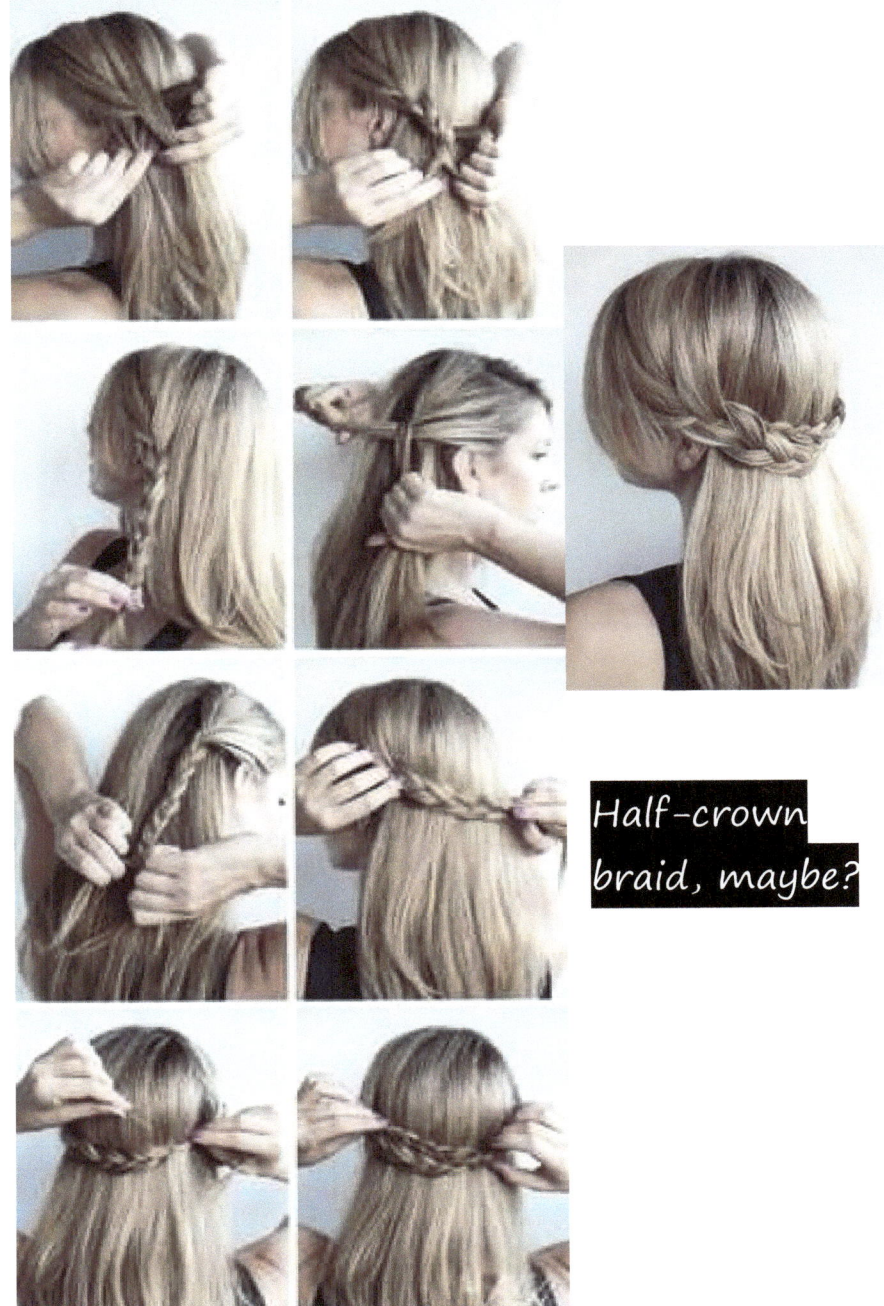

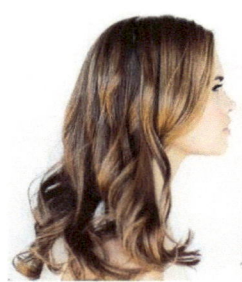
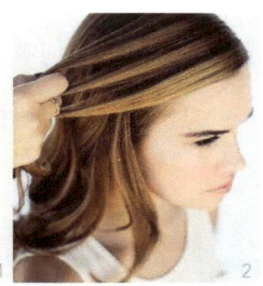
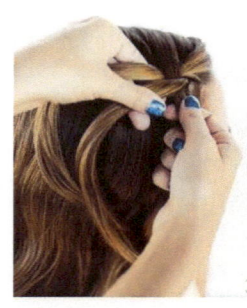
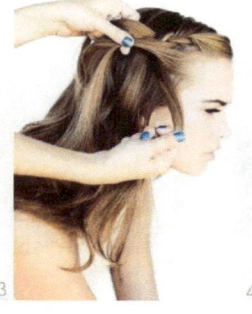

When life doesn't allow you to change anything else ..

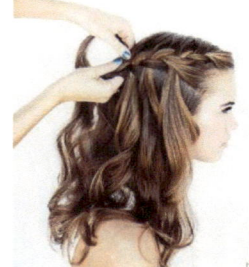
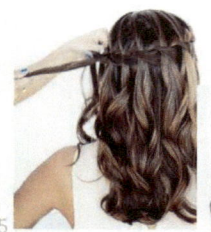
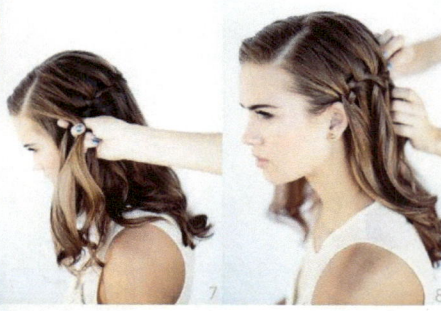

Get a new hairstyle

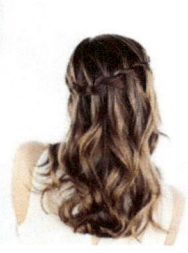
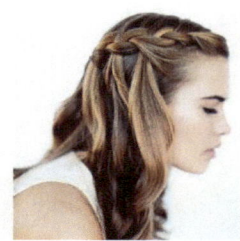

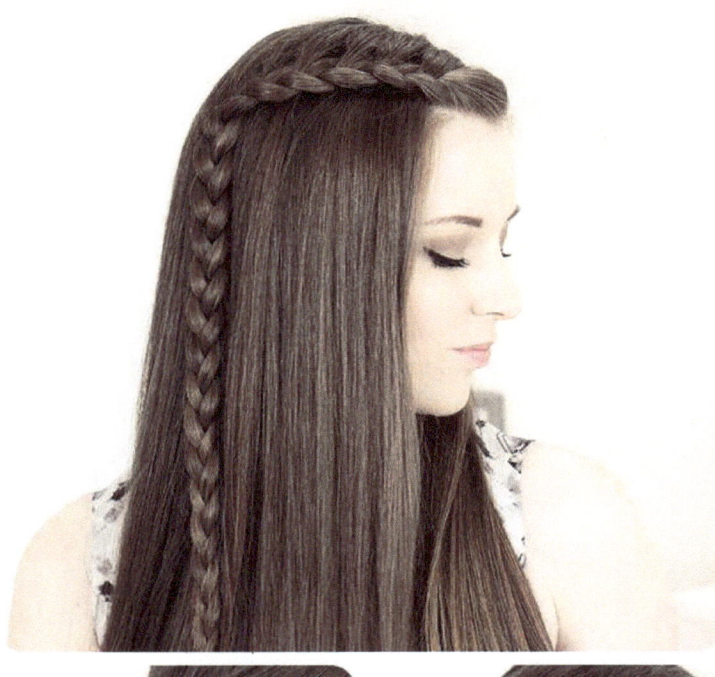
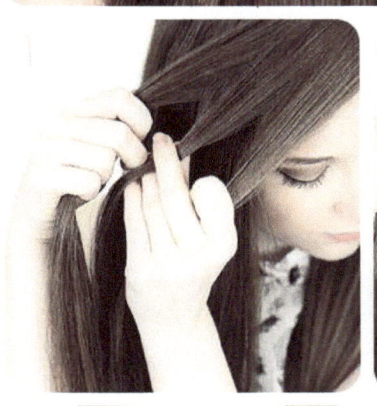
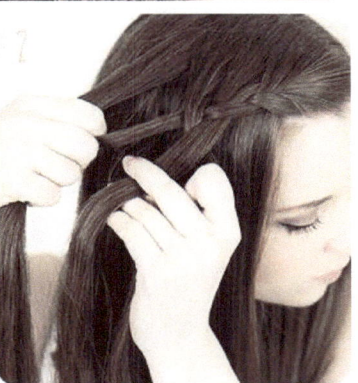
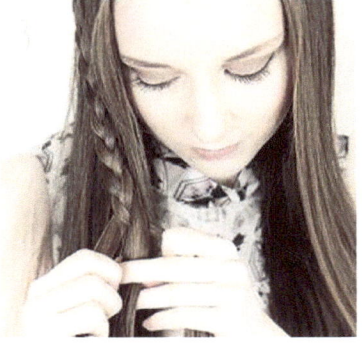
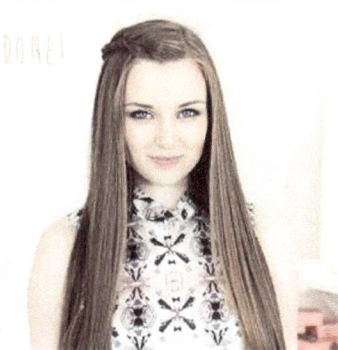

SIDE BRAIDS

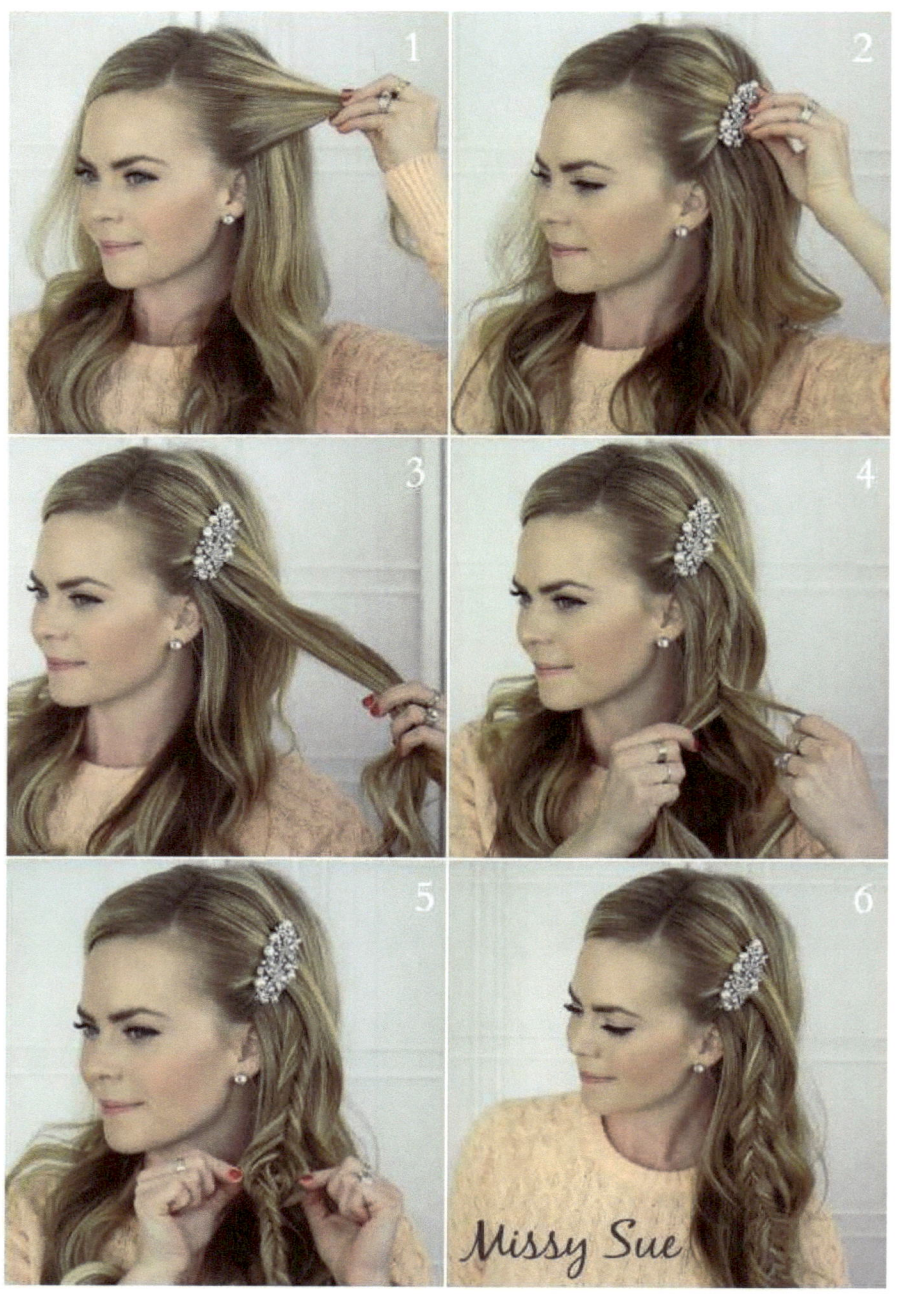

Embellished Fishtail Braid

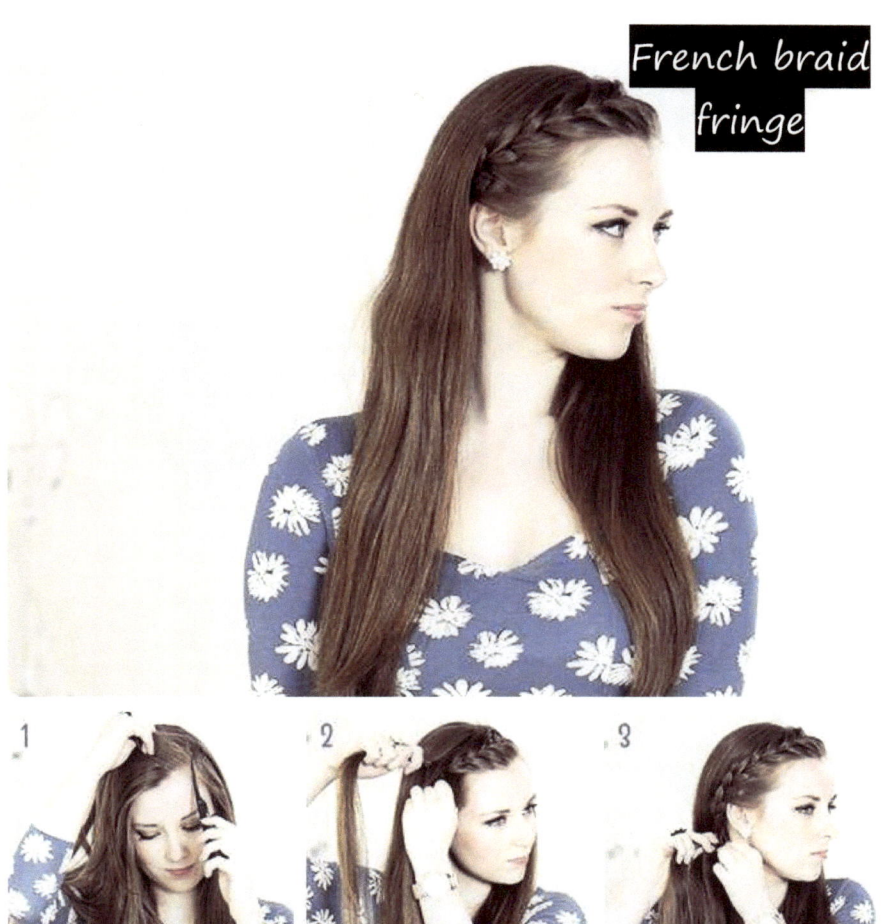

French braid fringe

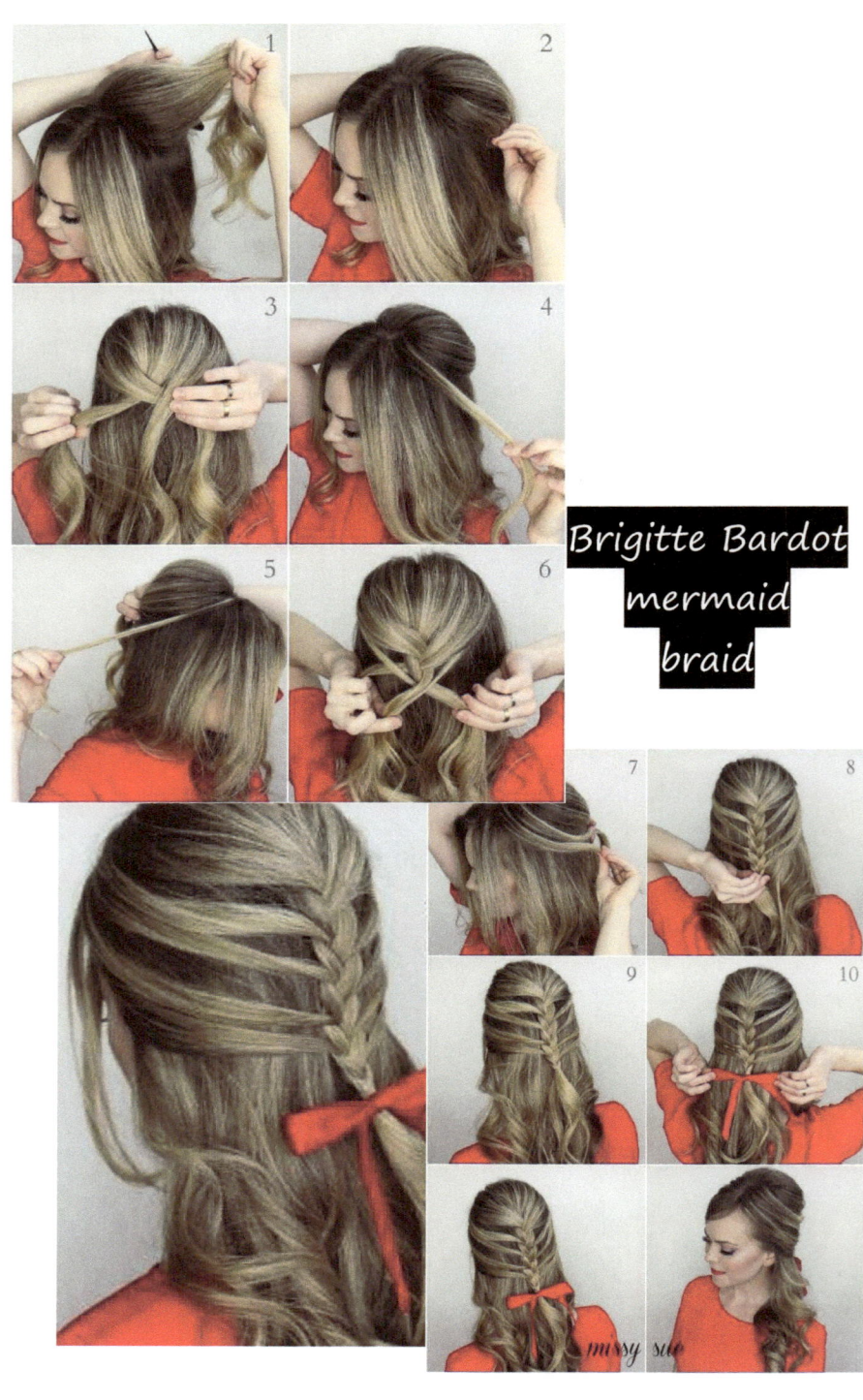

Brigitte Bardot mermaid braid

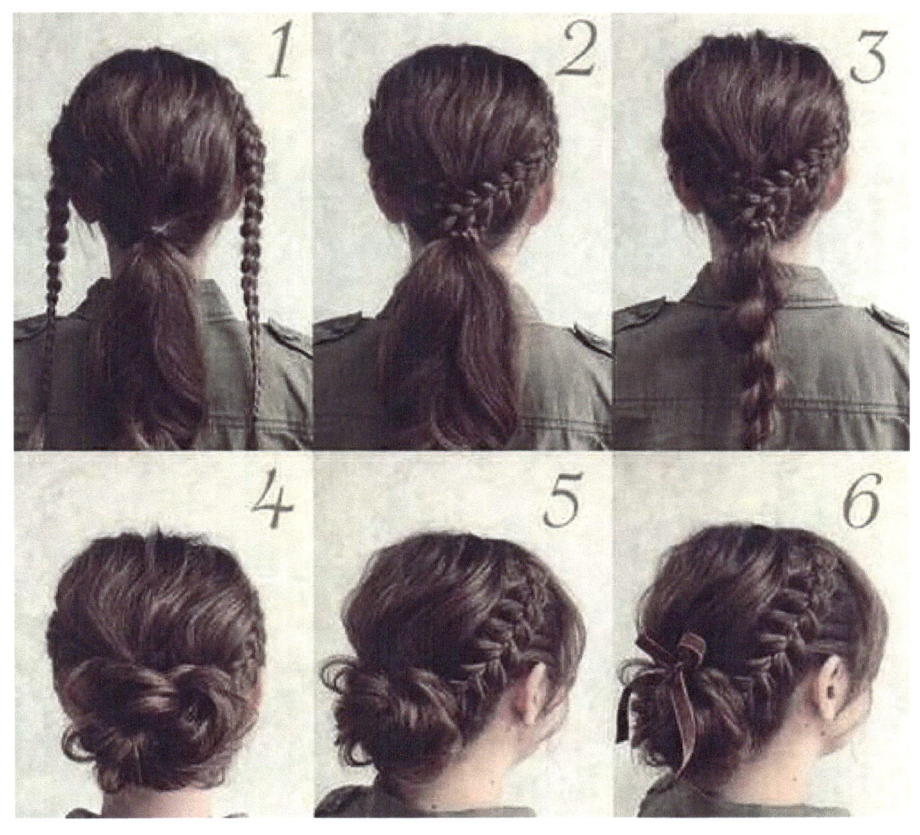

Sometimes, we just want to make a bun .. but a creative one though

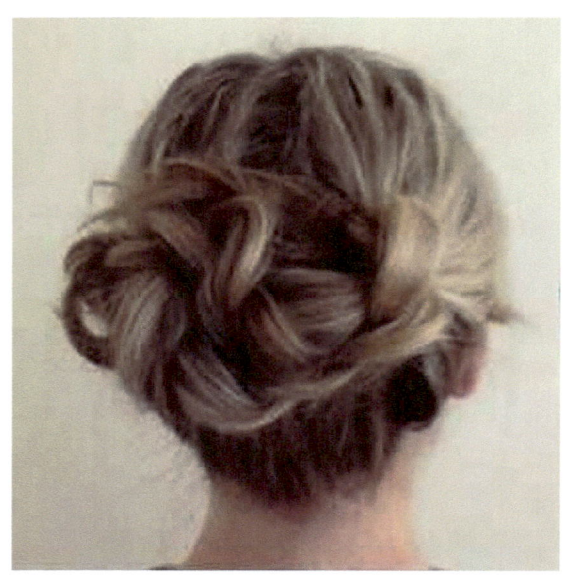

Easy twisted bun?

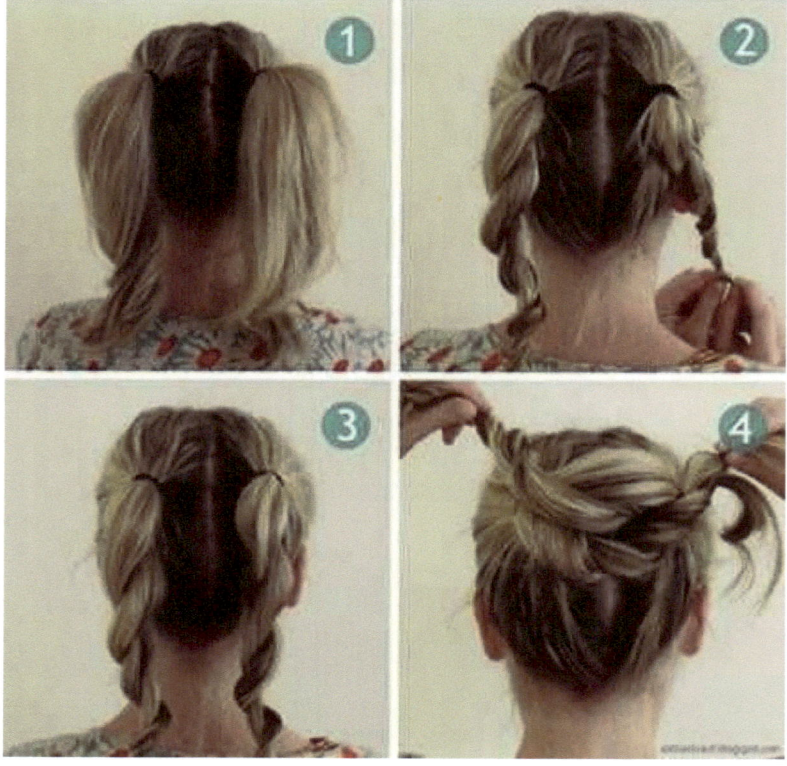

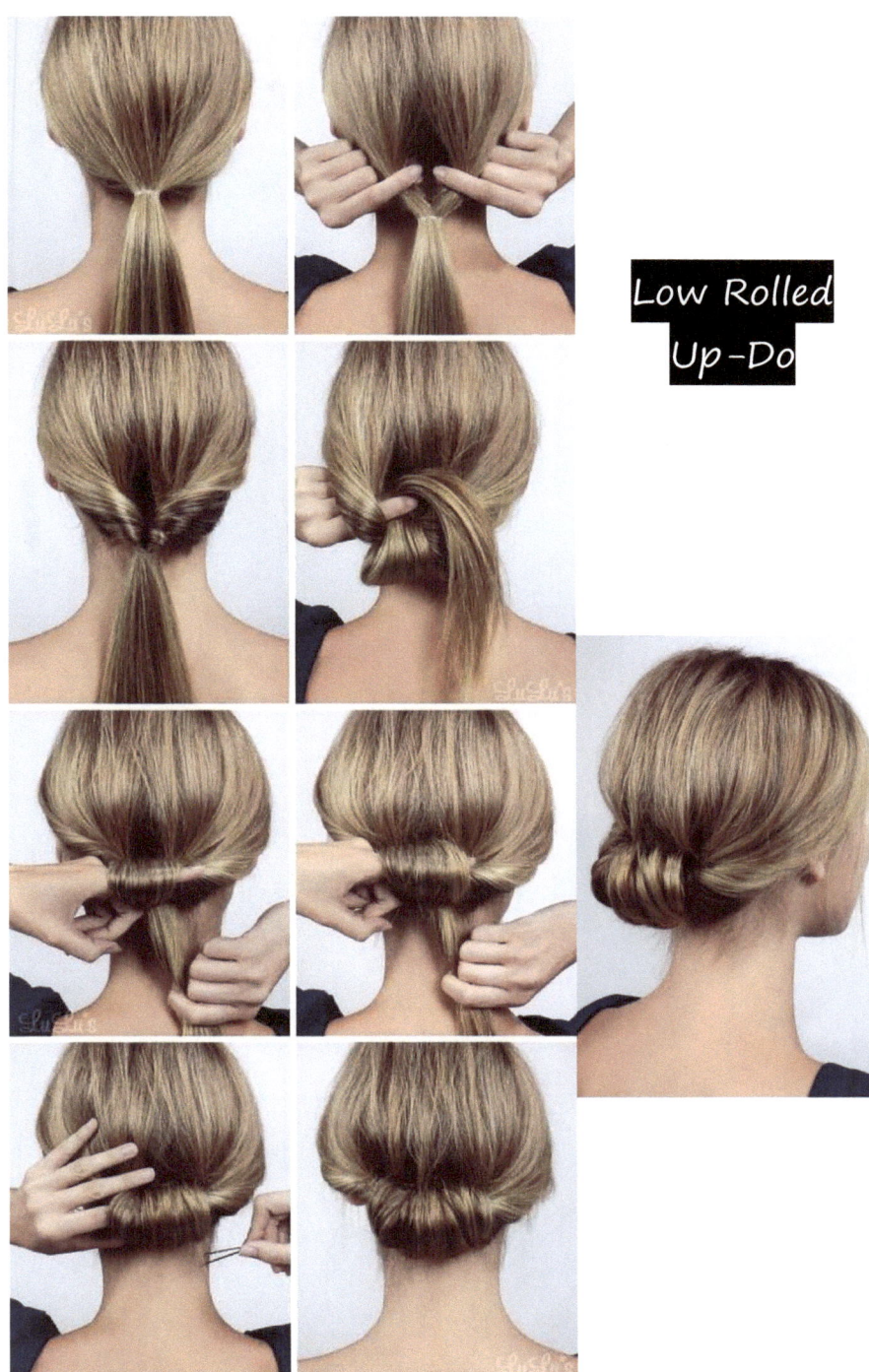

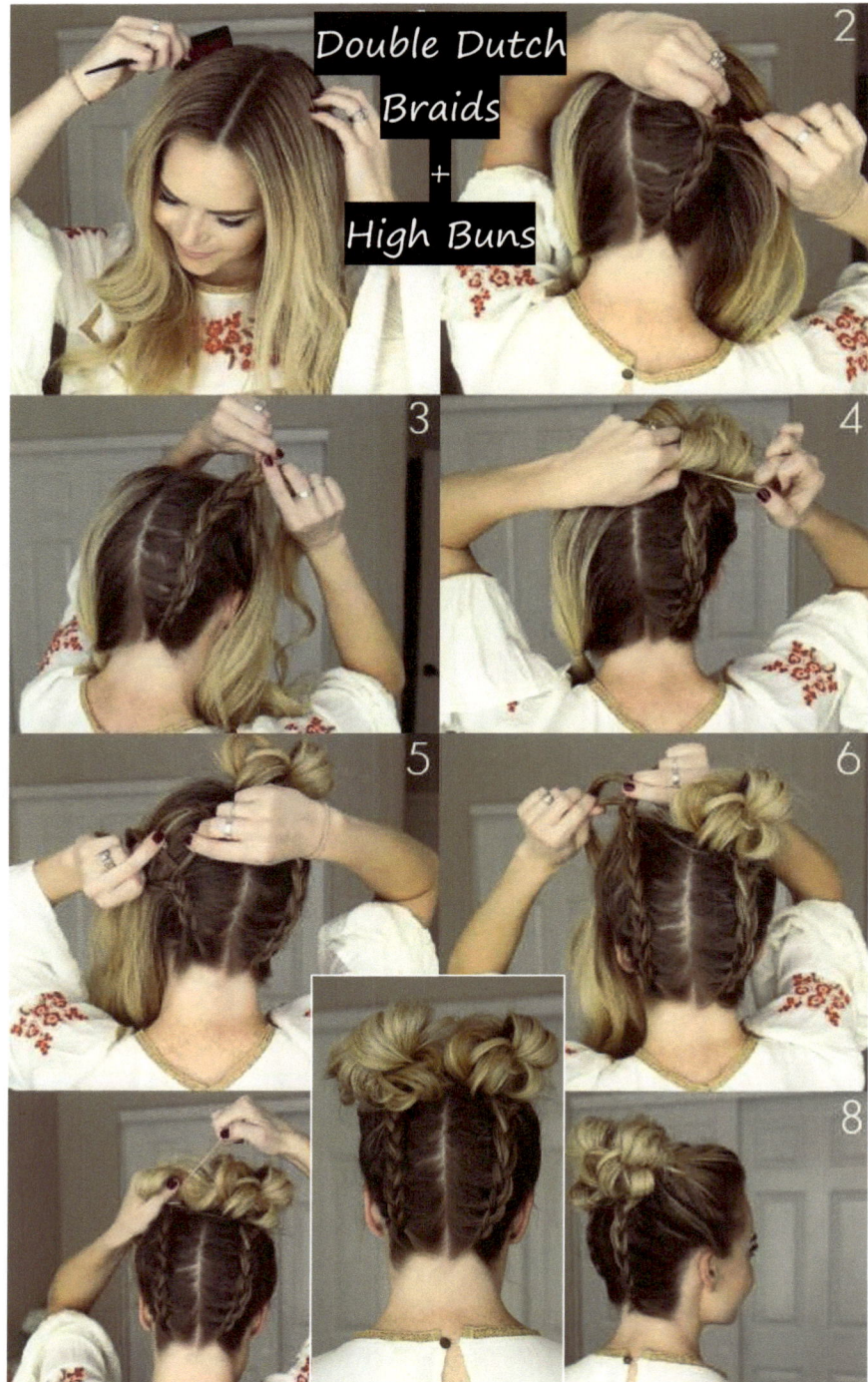

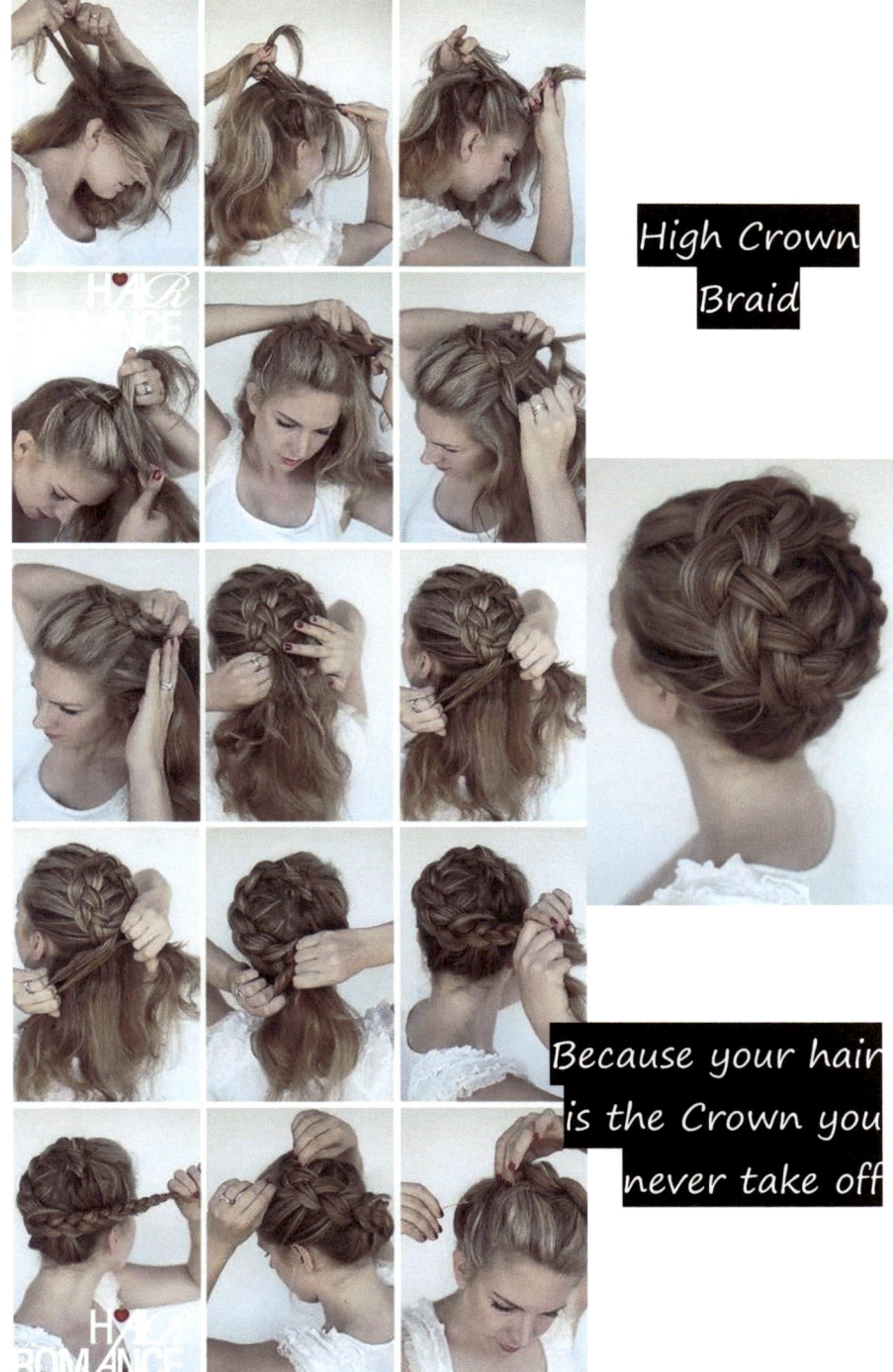

High Crown Braid

Because your hair is the Crown you never take off

# Easy Plaited Up-Do

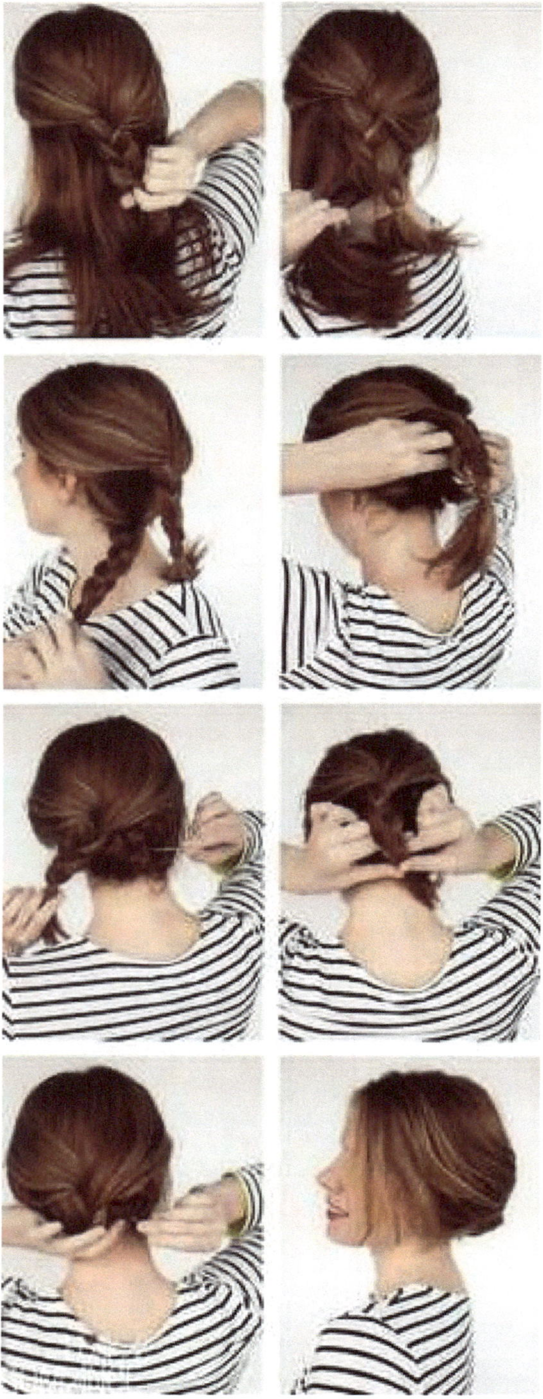

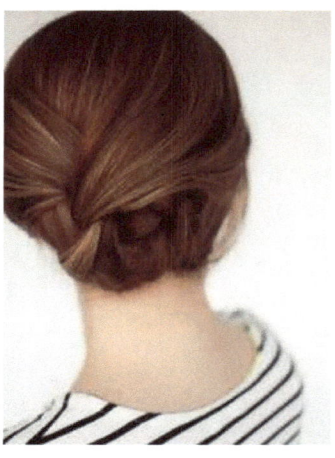

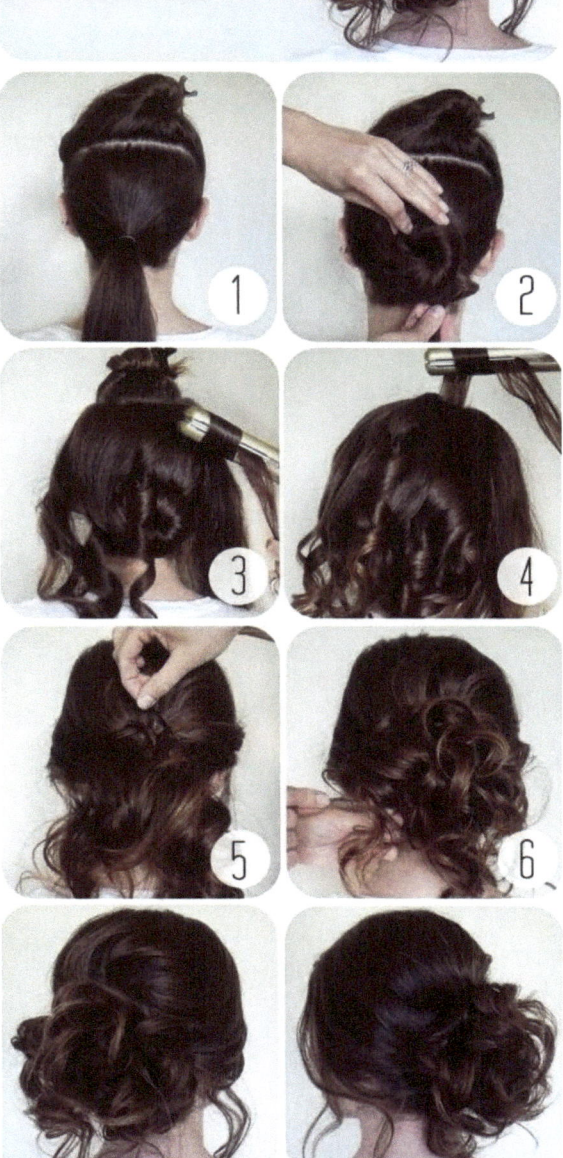

A new hairstyle is like a new relationship..

It makes you giddy, confident and excited.

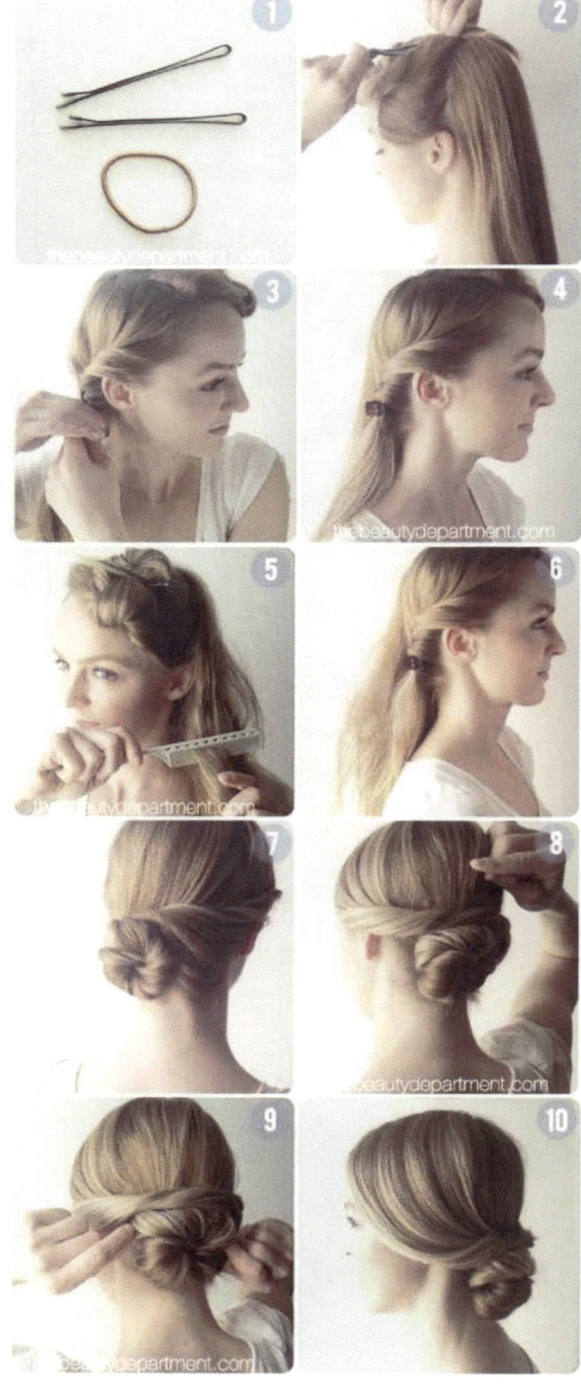

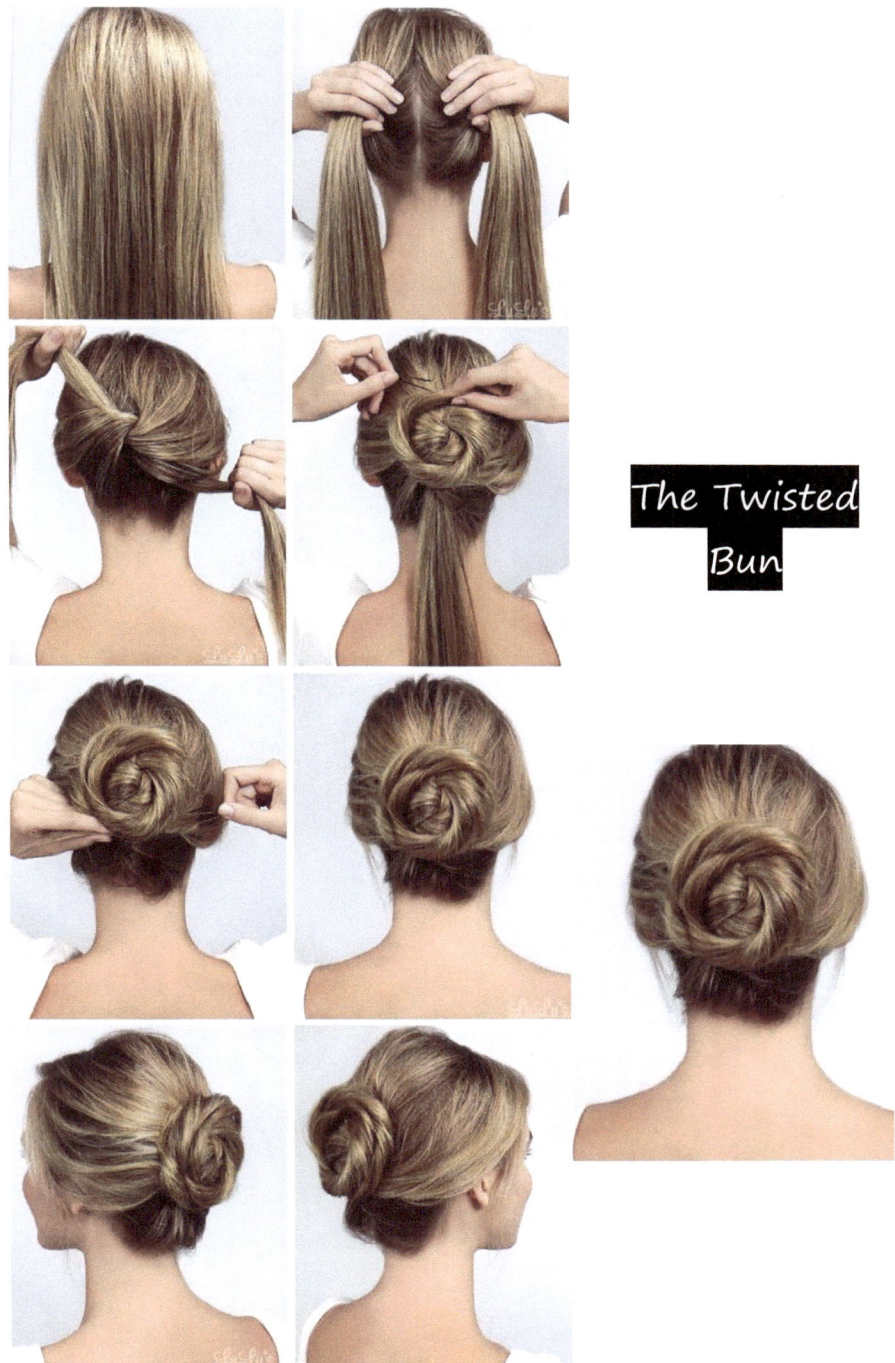

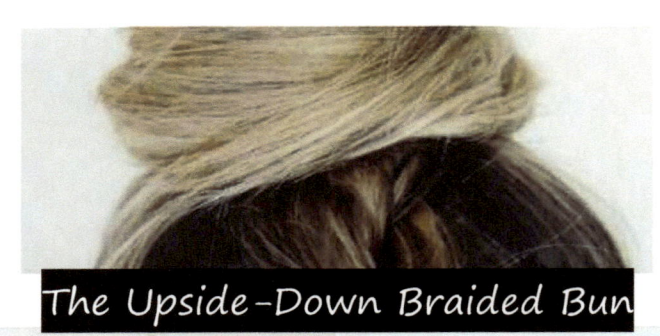

## The Upside-Down Braided Bun

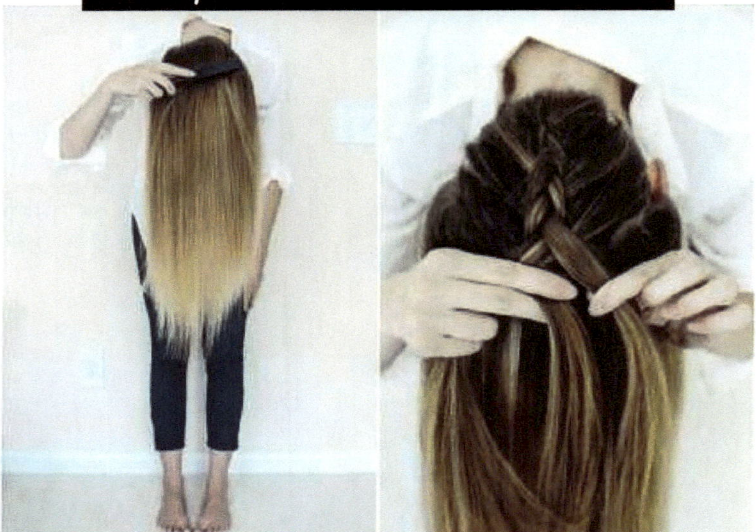

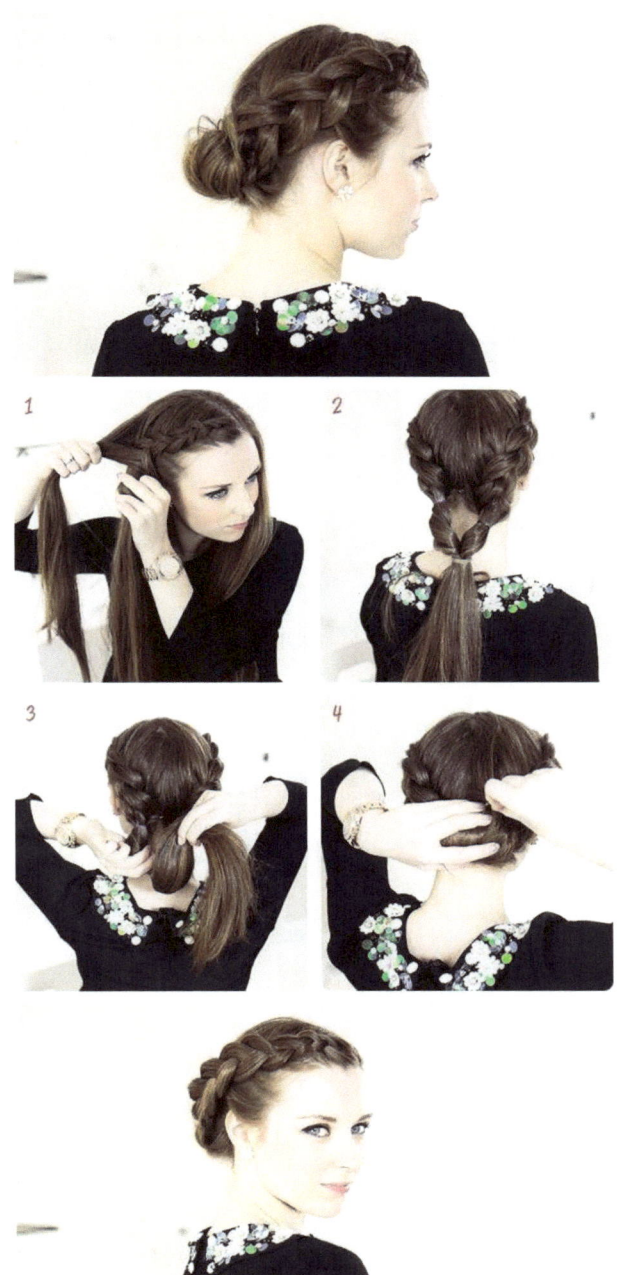

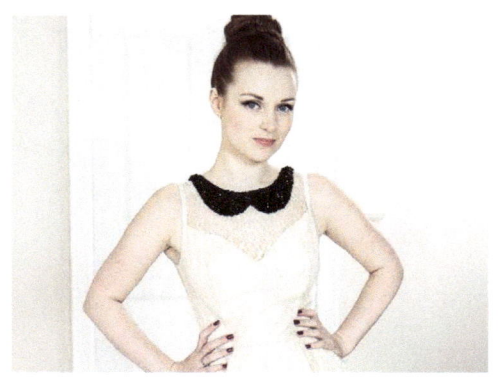
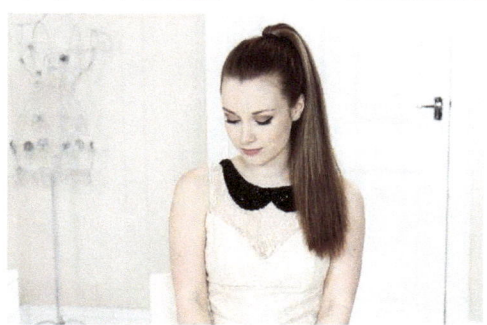
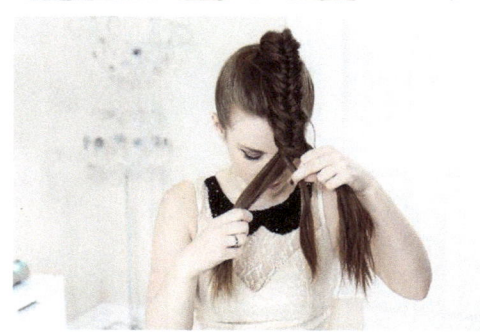
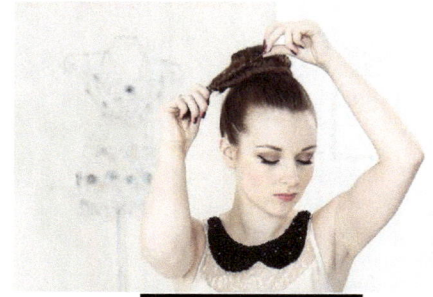

Fishtail Bun

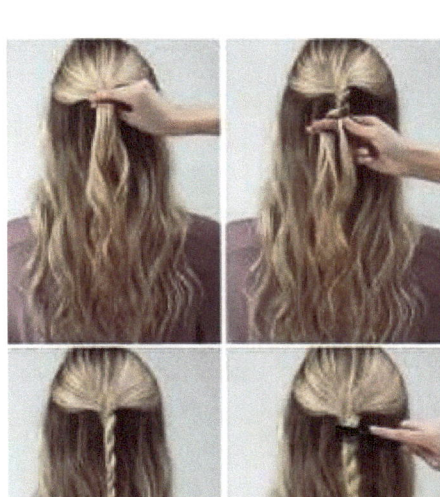

# Sweetheart Up-Do

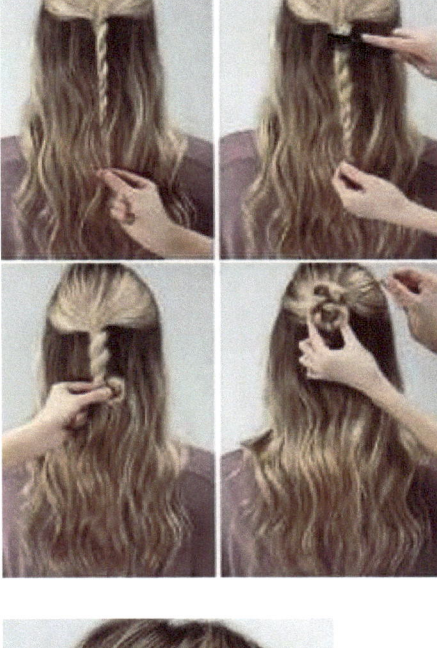
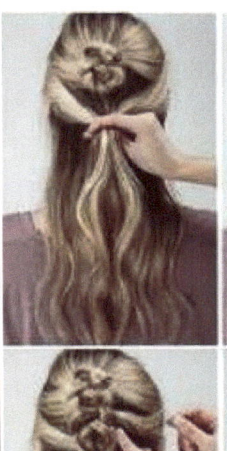
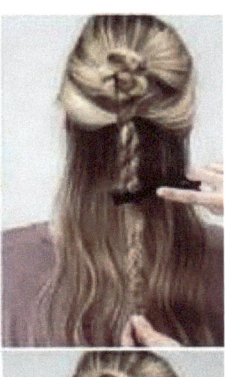
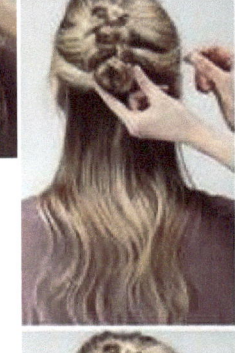
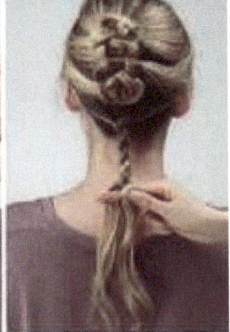
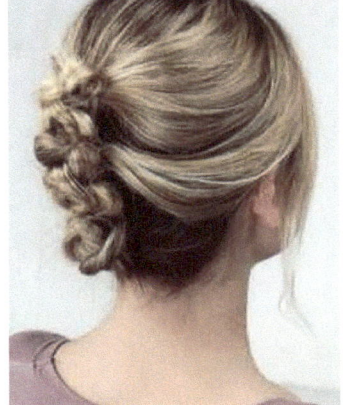
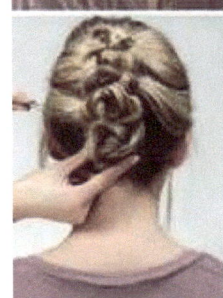
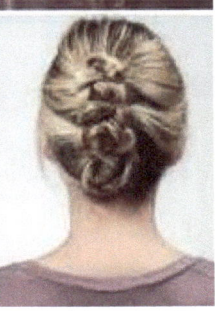

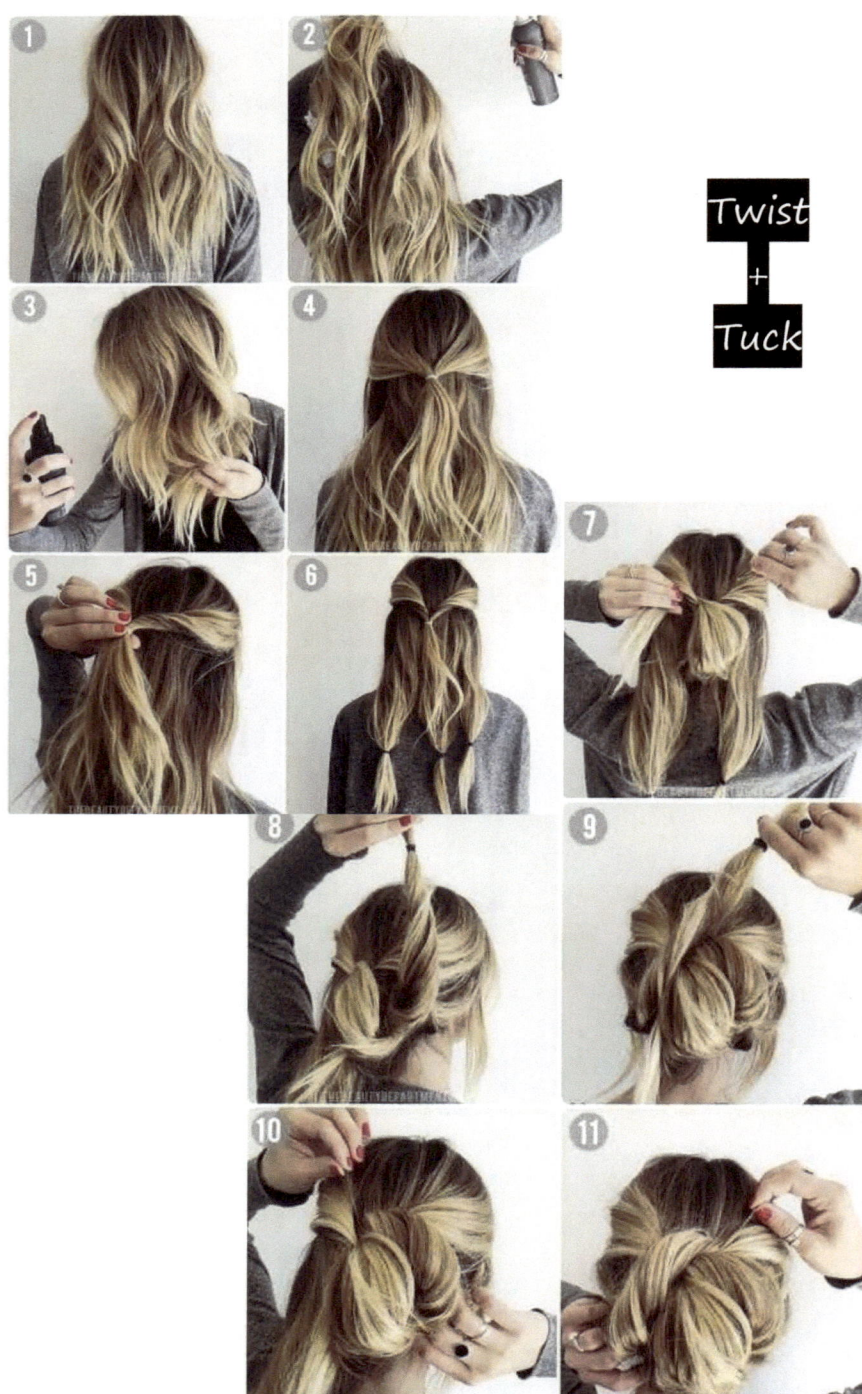

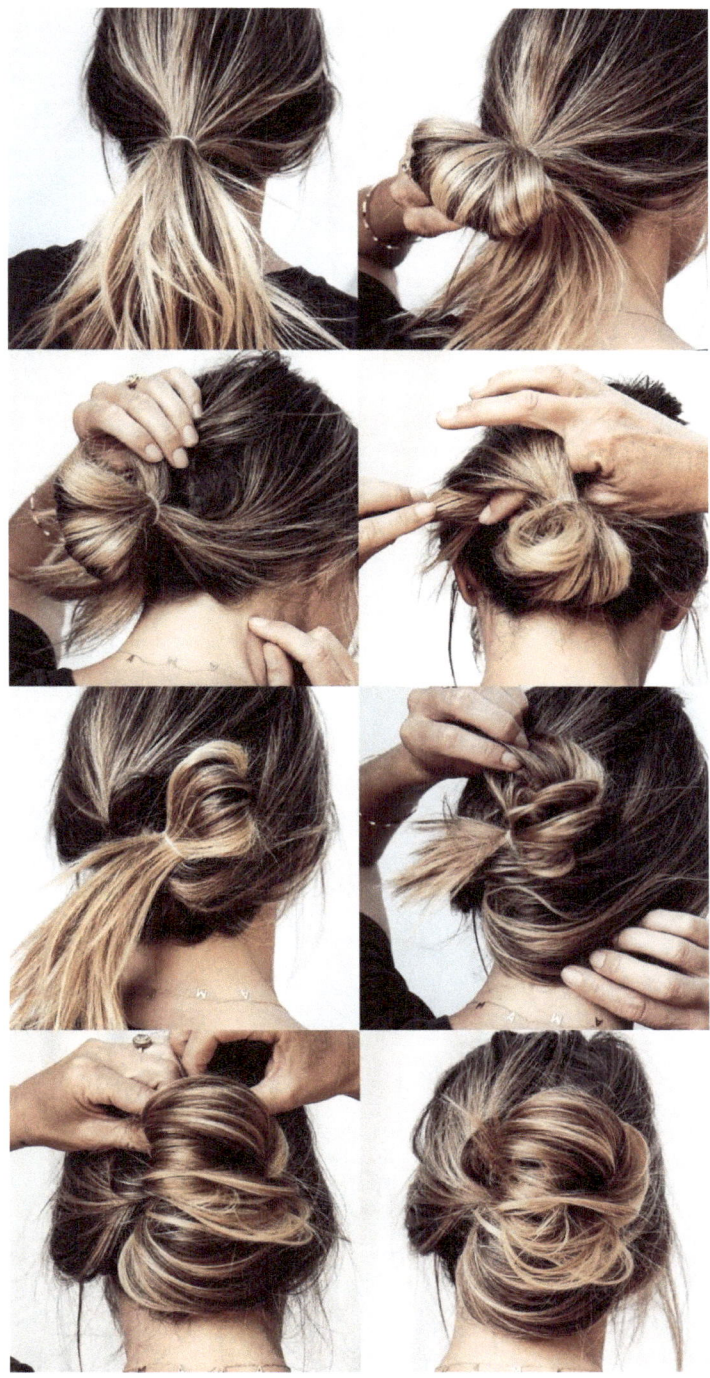

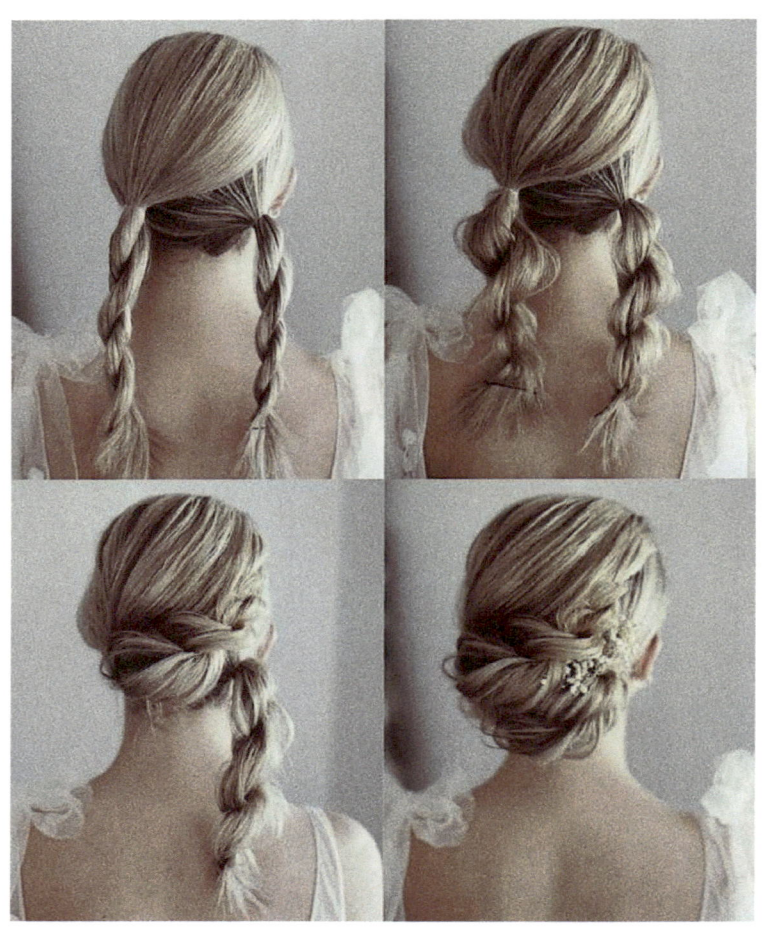

A change
in a hair style
Gives a new look

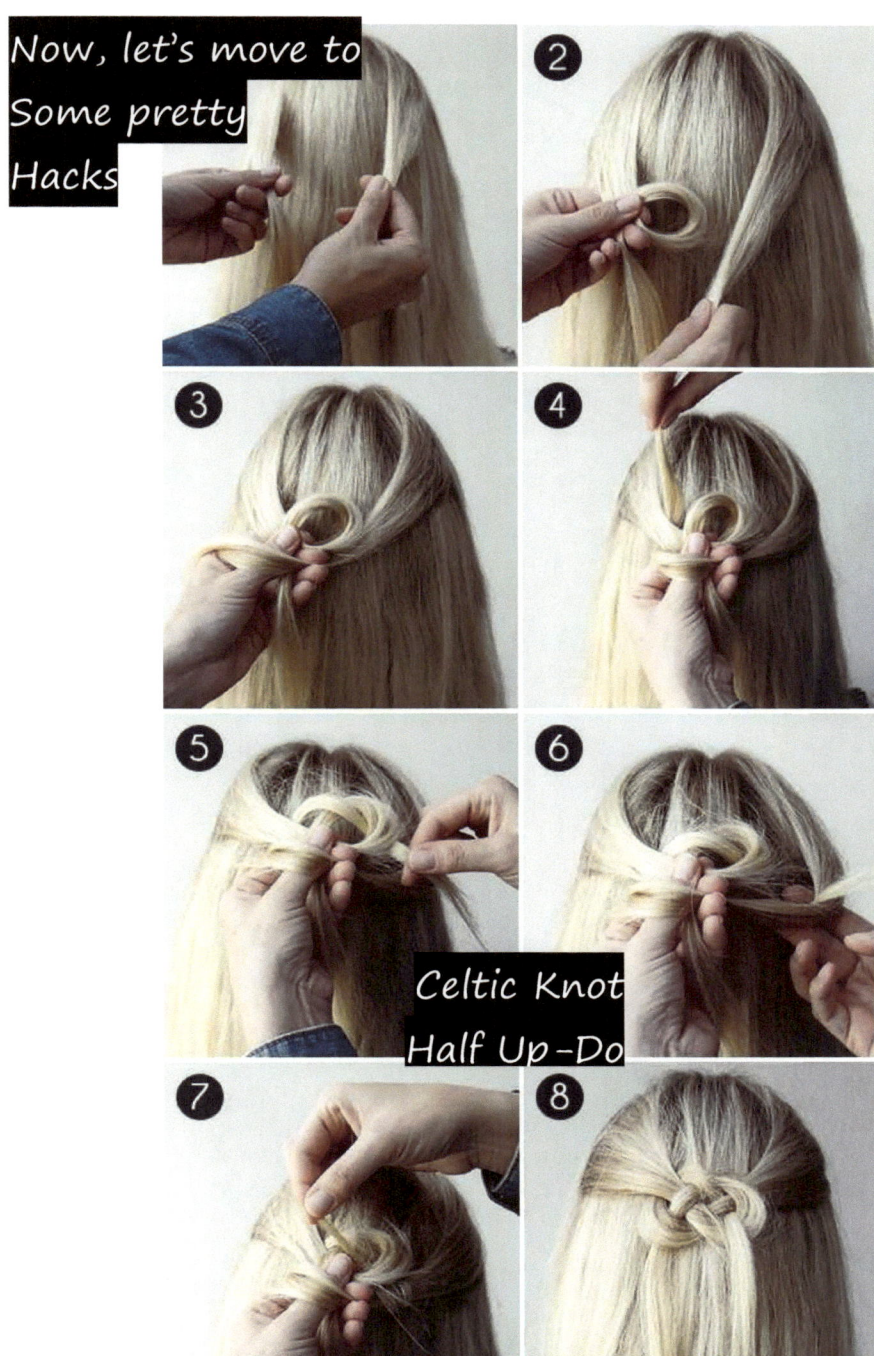

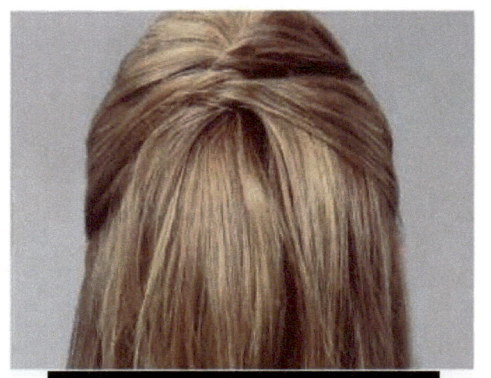

## Criss-Cross Half-Up

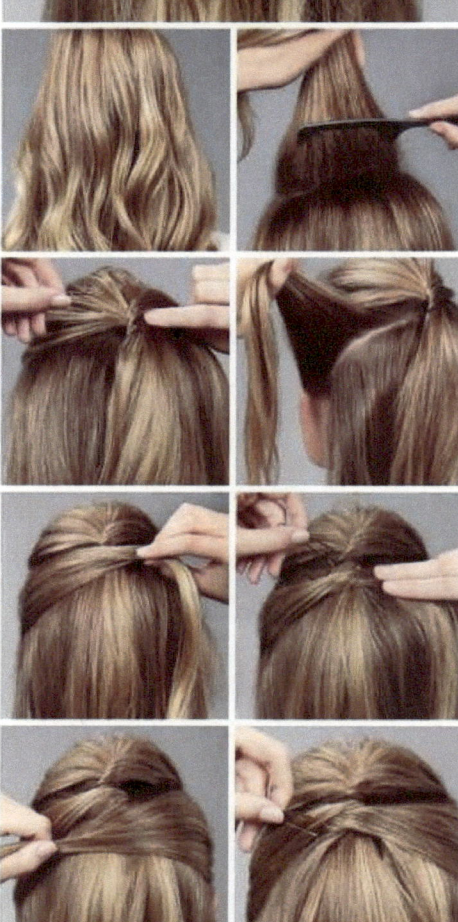

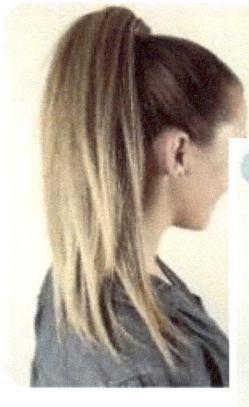

## The perfect Ponytail

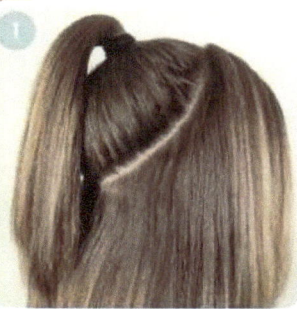
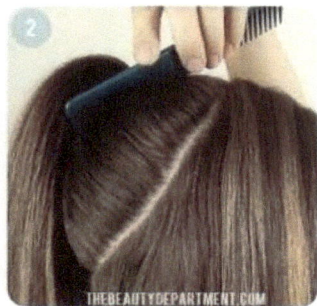
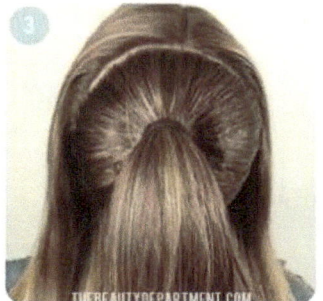
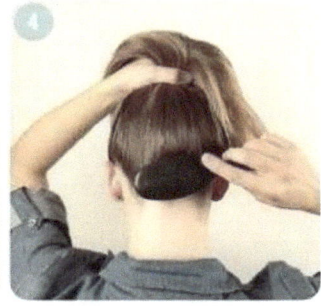
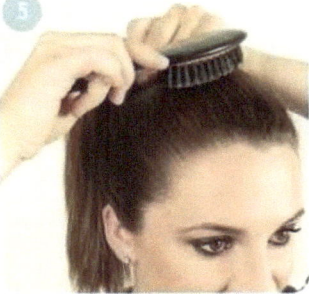
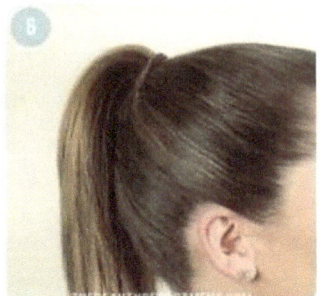
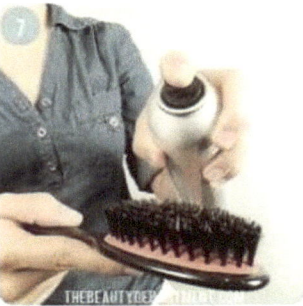
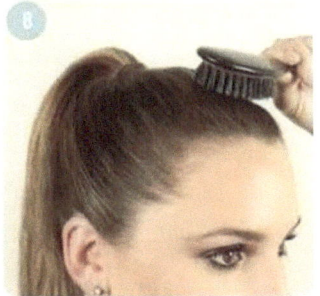

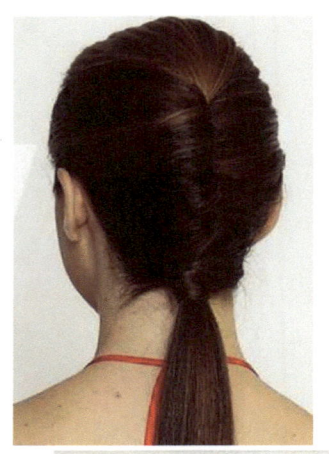

Sleek Vixen Hair

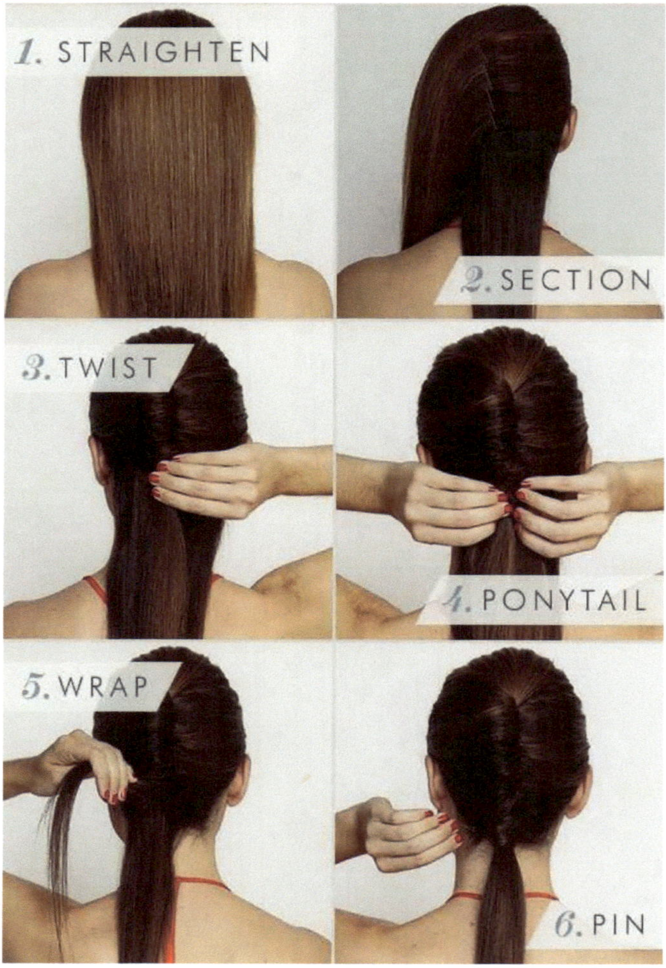

1. STRAIGHTEN
2. SECTION
3. TWIST
4. PONYTAIL
5. WRAP
6. PIN

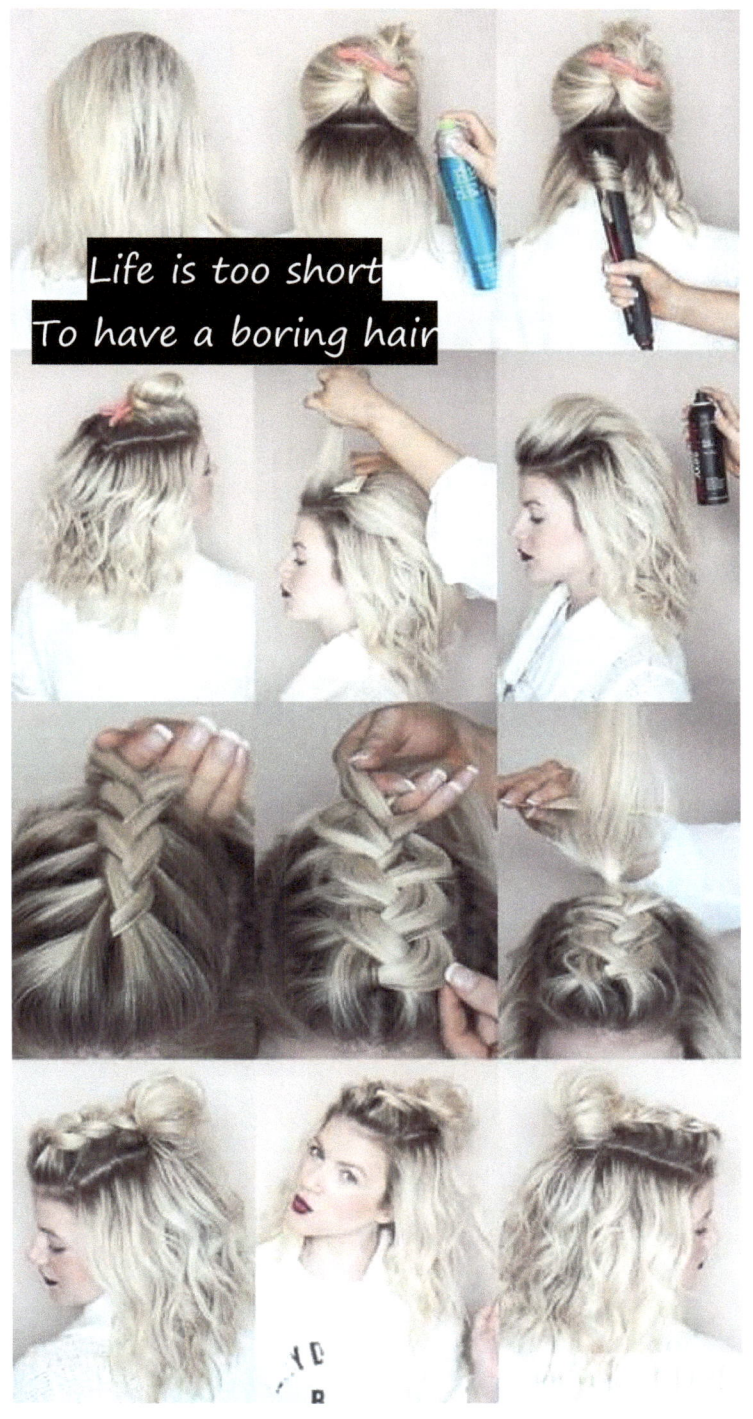

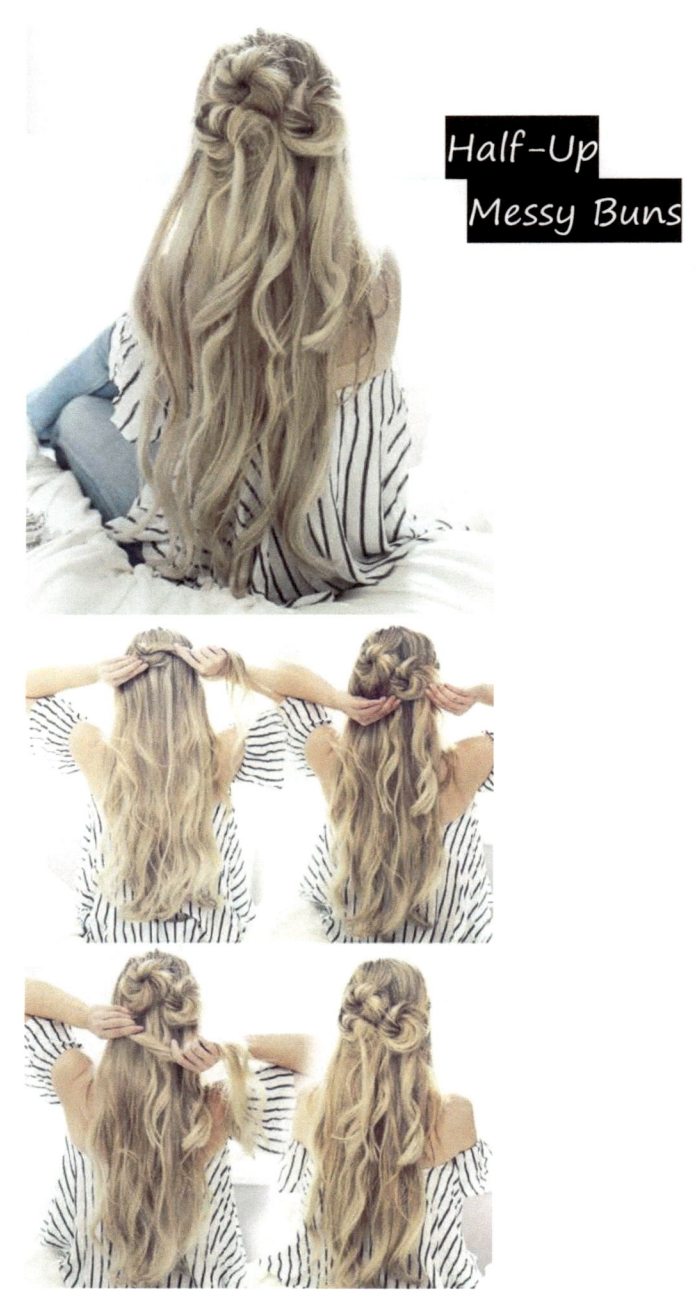

Half-Up Messy Buns

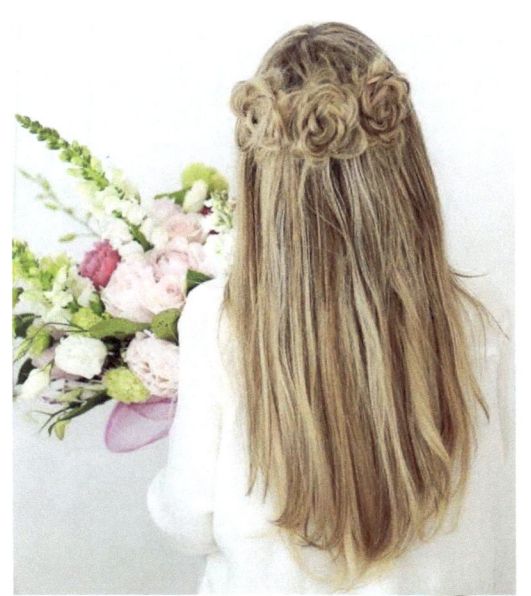

# Braided Flower Crown

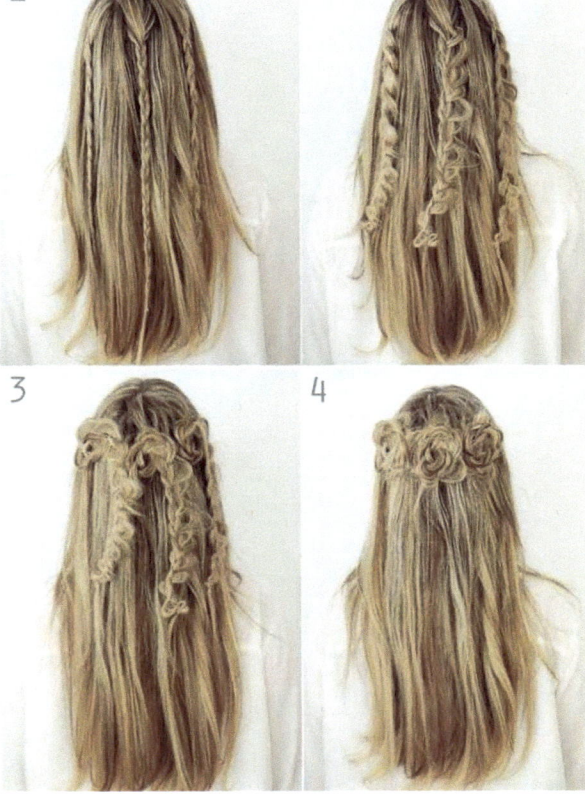

# Flip Twist Ponytail

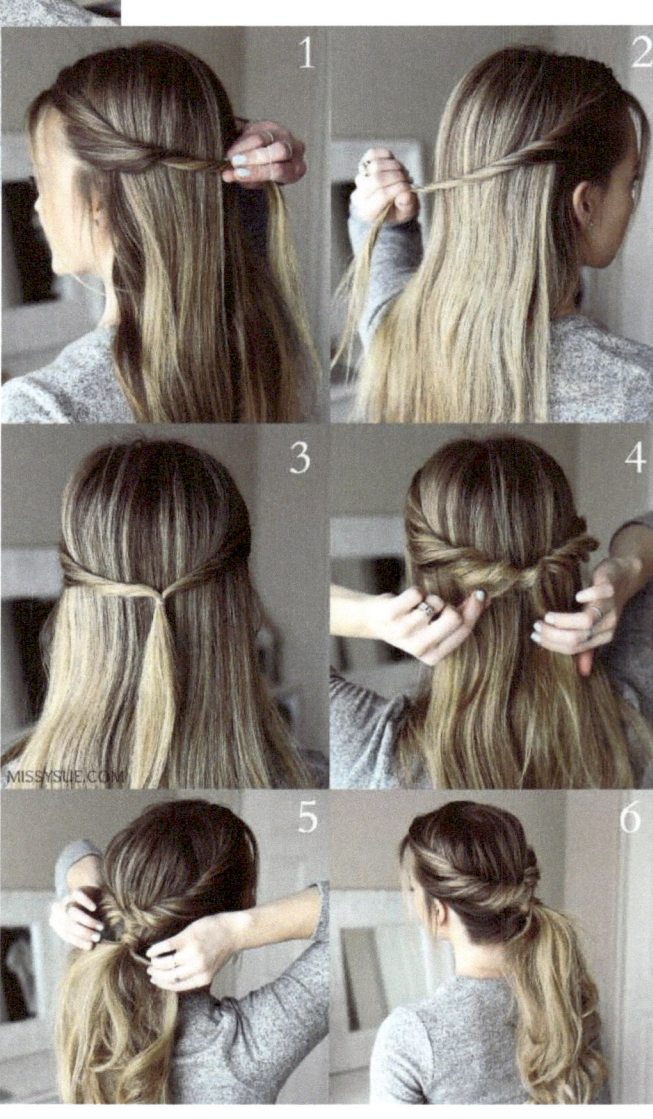

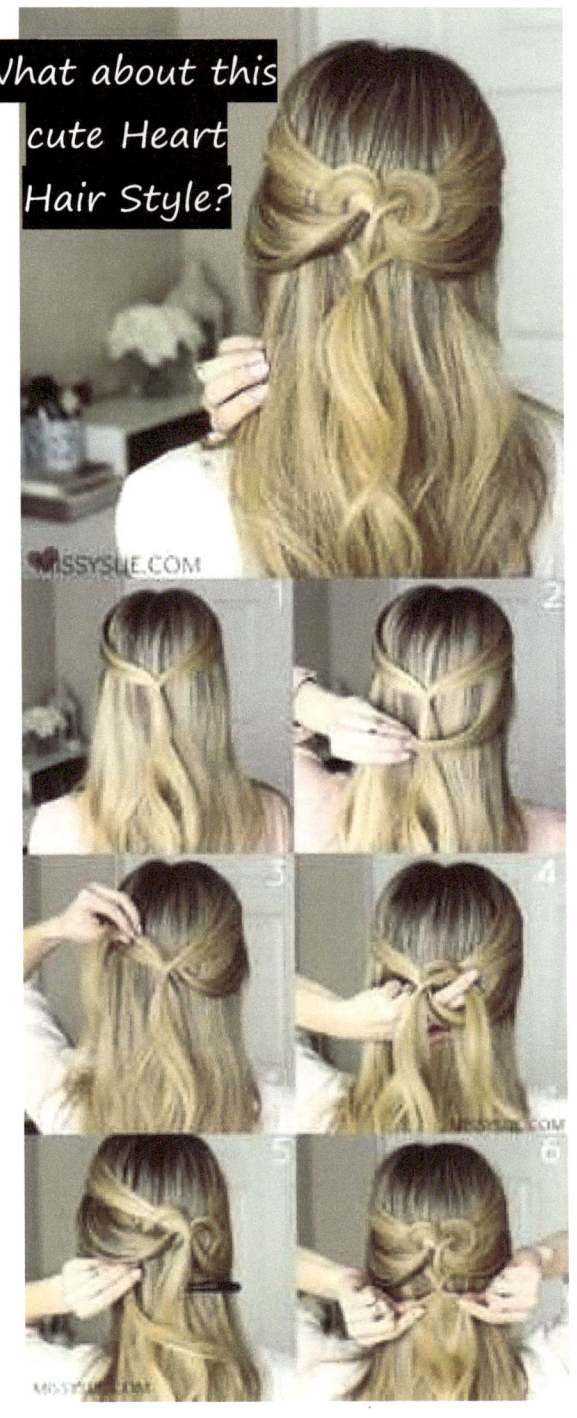

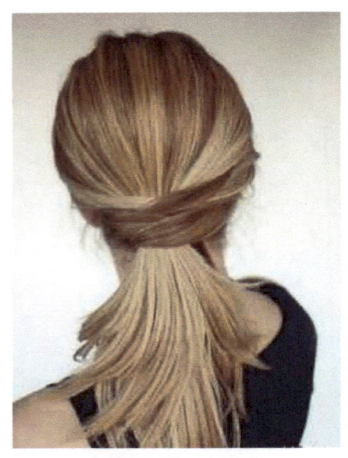

Chic Twisted Pony

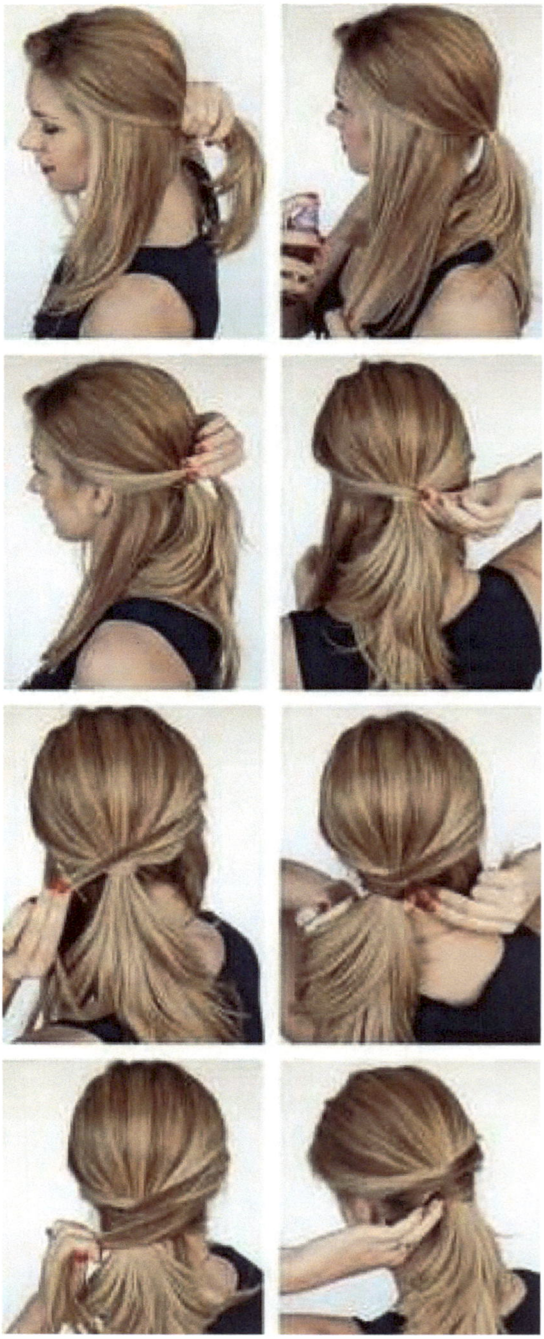

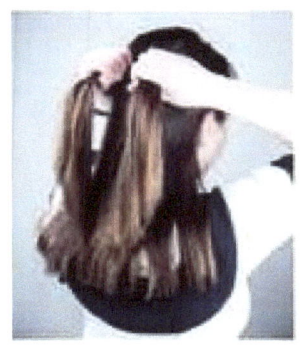 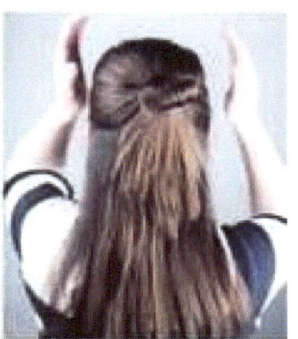
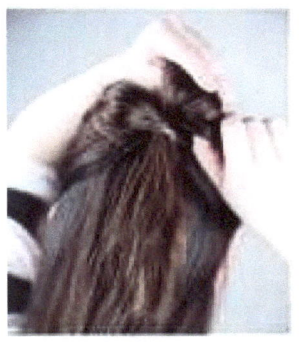 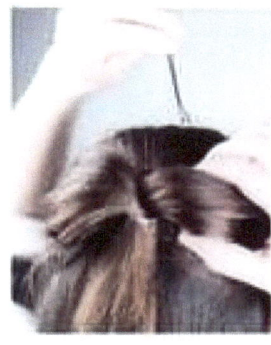
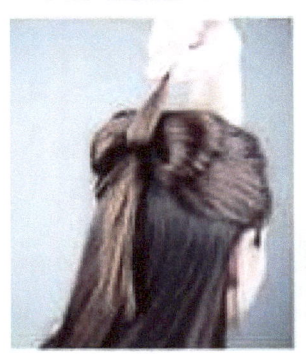 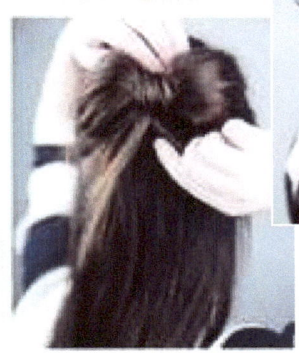
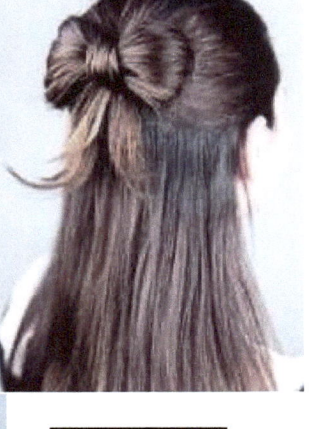
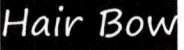
Hair Bow
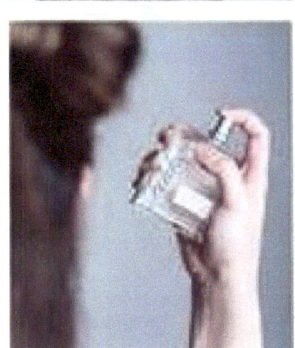 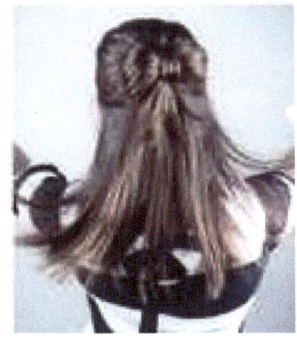

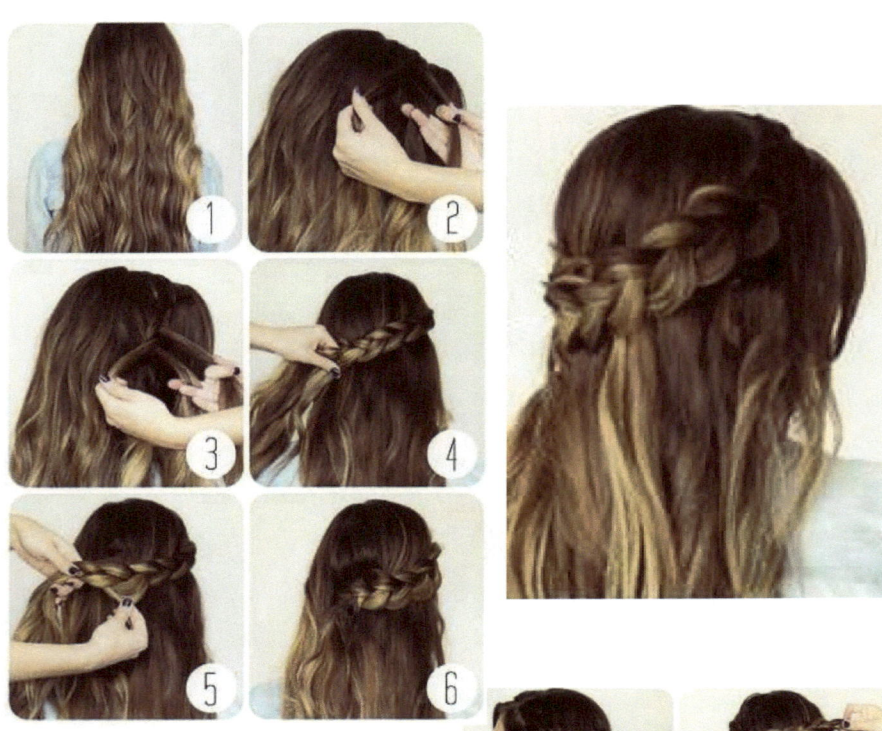

Wrap around Braid

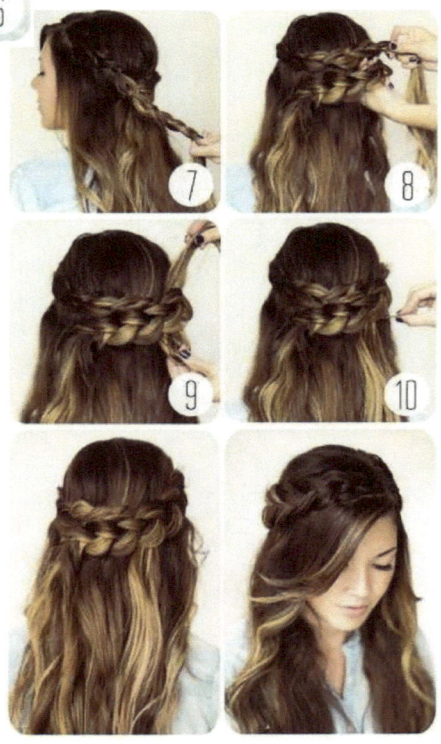

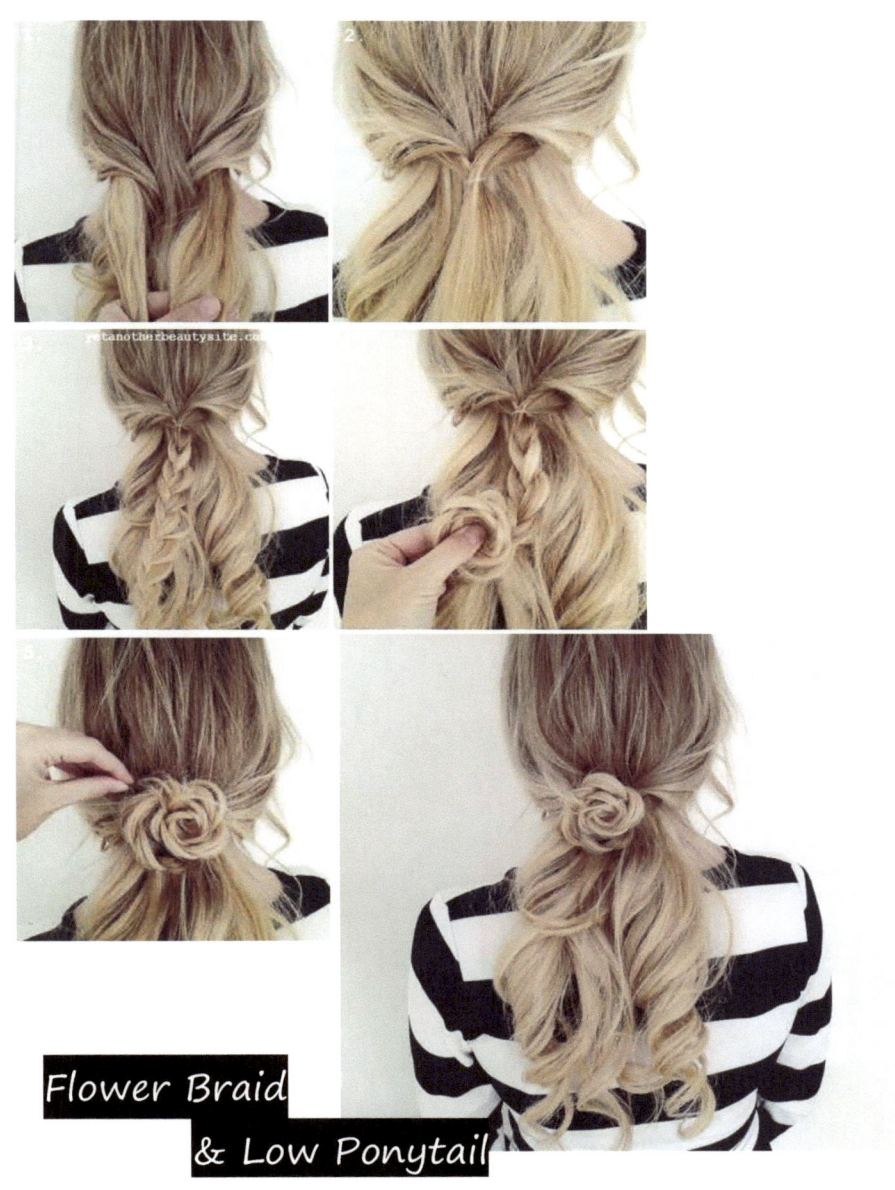

**Flower Braid & Low Ponytail**

Ordering this book means you got style
Made with love

www.ingramcontent.com/pod-product-compliance
Lightning Source LLC
Chambersburg PA
CBHW040334220526
45473CB00009B/2680